Rosie Ayliffe is the mother of Mia Ayliffe-Chung, who was killed at Home Hill Hostel in Townsville, Australia, in 2016. She is a former teacher, travel writer and journalist.

far from home

ROSIE AYLIFFE

VIKING
an imprint of
PENGUIN BOOKS

VIKING

UK | USA | Canada | Ireland | Australia
India | New Zealand | South Africa | China

Viking is part of the Penguin Random House group of companies whose
addresses can be found at global.penguinrandomhouse.com.

Penguin
Random House
Australia

First published by Viking, 2021

Cover design by Louisa Maggio © Penguin Random House Australia Pty Ltd
Text design by Midland Typesetters, Australia
Typeset in Adobe Garamond by Midland Typesetters, Australia
Every effort has been made to trace creators and copyright holders of the
photographic material included in this book. The publisher welcomes
hearing from anyone not correctly acknowledged.

Printed and bound in Australia by Griffin Press, part of Ovato, an accredited
ISO ANZ/NZS 14001 Environmental Management Systems printer

A catalogue record for this
book is available from the
National Library of Australia

ISBN 978 0 14379 639 8

penguin.com.au

MIX
Paper from
responsible sources
FSC® C009448

Dedicated to Mia, our one and only, our brave adventurer.
Always in our hearts.

Contents

1	Beginnings	1
2	Country Life	31
3	Mia's Early Travels	49
4	To Fall or Fly	59
5	88 Days and Counting	69
6	Mia's Death	75
7	Tributes	85
8	Bringing Mia Home	91
9	Memorials	99
10	Embarking on the Campaign Trail	103
11	Downtime	129
12	Turnbull and Trump	139
13	*Australian Story*	151
14	Going to Air	177
15	Surviving the Grief	191
16	Campaigning On – A Modern Slavery Act	203
17	Christmas	223
18	The Hearing	229
19	Festival of Light	243
	Postscript	251
	Acknowledgements	255
	Resources	257

1

Beginnings

THE TWO POLICEMEN ARRIVED AT AROUND 10 PM, JUST AS WE WERE thinking about turning in. The news they gave me was to destroy my world and take away my whole reason for being, but I didn't know that as I answered the door. In fact, I invited them in and offered them a cup of tea, as if they were friends.

Wondering whether we'd left the garage door open again, I studied their faces. From their serious demeanour I could tell that wasn't it. Maybe one of the dogs had got into the neighbour's chickens?

They declined the tea and sat down. One of the men was incredibly young, while the other had a solid, reliable air about him. They were sitting on our new leather sofa, hemmed in somewhat by our curious dogs. Nancy the lurcher gazed in suspicion at the guy next to her, while Fynn, our young bearded collie, peered up from the floor, occasionally offering a paw to the younger policeman, who was trying to ignore him. It could have been worse: Fynn had been neutered a few days previously but had calmed down considerably, otherwise – as we reflected later – he would have been humping the guy's leg.

My partner Stewart and I had bought our 1940s ex-council house after the owner had passed away. We'd already spent the best part of a year living in and out of a caravan on the drive while Stewart knocked walls in, laid new floors throughout, replaced the kitchen, bathroom and all the doors, while I stripped off the 80s wallpaper, pulled up old carpets and removed 70s-style polystyrene ceiling tiles. The next job was to build an extension, an annexe which we hoped my daughter, Mia, would use for her planned business venture of a day nursery for toddlers.

We were happy with progress so far, but at this stage I was aware that things looked unfinished – the fireplace had no mantelpiece, and skirting boards weren't yet in place. 'What must these visitors be thinking of us?' I wondered.

But I saw that the police officers weren't paying attention to their surroundings. They both seemed shaken and subdued.

'There's no easy way to tell you this. Your daughter's been involved in an incident – she's been fatally wounded.'

It took me a moment to process this.

'You mean she's dead?'

Mia was born in South London, too far from the sound of Bow Bells to be a true cockney, on 7 October 1995. To my surprise she came out perfect, as clean as a pin, without a speck of blood or mucus anywhere. Throughout my pregnancy I had been steeling myself, fully expecting something to go wrong before the birth, or for the baby to have health issues. I suppose I didn't think I was worthy of a child this perfect. From day one, I was smitten.

Mia's father, Howard, had three girls by a previous marriage. By the time Mia was born they were in their teens, and he was a far more experienced parent than I was. But, to be honest, from the very beginning Mia seemed to need very little by way of expertise in parenting: she latched on immediately, and after I brought her home during a freak October snow storm she just seemed to want to sleep interminably. I hadn't been expecting this at all!

Howard took Mia to the register office, with strict instructions to record her double-barrelled surname. However, I had been less specific about her Christian names, and so she ended up with a string which was to plague medical records and school registers for the rest of her life: Mia Mishka (a name we'd toyed with instead of Mia) Annie (after my maternal grandma) Josephine (after Howard's maternal grandma) Ayliffe-Chung. At that point in time it took up more of a page than she did. This irritated the hell out of me, but Mia absolutely loved it when she was older and taught all her friends to chant it like some kind of mantra.

I'd read book after book about parenting and they all mentioned sleeplessness in the early days. Mia could sleep for nineteen hours at a stretch, leaving me at something of a loose end, with little to do except to study yet more parenting books. She was so unresponsive to noises that eventually the health visitor decided Mia needed a hearing check. The prognosis was . . . perfect hearing – she was just a very chilled-out baby, which was jokingly ascribed to her Jamaican heritage. However, I think it may have had something to do with on-demand feeding and keeping her beside us at all times during those early days. Basically, Mia was either on the hip or on the breast, or in a bed in the living room or in bed with Howard and me, for the entirety of her first year.

Mia's heritage, of which she became very proud, was English on my side, and Jamaican-Chinese on her father's. In many people's eyes, the Chinese minority in Jamaica became all too successful in business in Jamaica (as the Chinese diaspora has tended to be worldwide), controlling 90 per cent of dried goods stores and supermarkets by the 1960s. As a result, they were subjected to a wave of interracial violence and many fled for their lives, including Howard's family, losing all their land and property in the process. This was a source of some bitterness in the community, and I remember being surprised at Howard actually welling up when he explained the situation to me, but happily members of Howard's family had since returned to settle on the island.

My family was delighted to welcome Mia, as although I was the third of four children, Mia was the first grandchild. For a brief spell I basked in the glory of being favoured by my parents, and Mum went to the length of knitting Mia a beautiful little sweater with an intricate lacy collar. Mum's work commitments as a teacher had prevented her from knitting like this for us when we were youngsters – and what she had produced when Ruth and I were toddlers had been basic items which were, frankly, quite ugly – so I was deeply moved by the work and effort that had gone into this pretty garment, and what it said about her devotion to the new addition to the family. As a non-churchgoer I'd been the black sheep of our family for years, so this was a new experience for all of us! Mia fulfilled the desire for a new life, someone to carry on the family genes. It was Dad who'd asked for her surname to include our surname Ayliffe, which Howard and I were very happy to do. And Mia Mishka Annie Josephine Ayliffe-Chung was loved by all.

*

When Mia was about three months old, Mum, Dad, Mia and I made the journey from London up to Yorkshire to see my child's great-grandmother, Annie. My dear and beloved maternal grandma had lived through poverty and hardship with a fortitude I had always admired. Born in 1907 and the fourth of five children, she never knew her own parents as she was adopted at the age of two by an uncle and aunt. Her mother, Jane Elizabeth, who'd worked in a bar before she was married, had taken her own life by drowning in 1909. Her husband had tried to save her, but she fought him off.

Annie's aunt was a hard taskmaster. She took Annie out of school at the age of twelve to work in the family dairy, a development that my mother found dubious, expressing to me her doubts about whether or not Annie was adopted in her own interests, given she was basically free labour. My sister Ruth recalls Annie describing how she used to scrub floors until her hands bled, and how, on the day of her wedding, she was required to complete her chores before being allowed to dress for the occasion. Years later in Australia when I met Aunty Jane and the Pacific Islanders and learnt of their experiences of enslavement, I immediately felt a sense of kinship with them because of Annie's difficult past.

In the 1950s and 60s my grandad Percy, Annie's husband, had worked in the coal mines as a weigh man, weighing bags of coal as they emerged from the depths. Because of his shift pattern he narrowly missed the Silverwood Pit disaster of 1966, when ten men died and twenty-nine were injured. He was there as the bodies emerged. Such events politicised a generation of workers, and the whole family were staunch unionists as a consequence.

Money was always a scarce commodity for the miners, although they did get free coal for life. Mum said she always wondered why Annie had never sat down with them at the table to eat, and only as an adult did she consider that perhaps there just wasn't enough food to go around, so her mum would eat whatever was left. Whether this was true or not, she had to be ordered to sit at the table even when I was a teenager and things were less difficult financially.

As a stalwart Methodist, Annie had taken the pledge and always had a fear and loathing of alcohol: my uncle remembers Grandad coming home with a bottle of beer one Christmas and Annie berating him angrily. In her later life, tiny and seemingly frail as a bird, she volunteered at the call centre for Samaritans, the charity for people struggling to cope and at risk of suicide, perhaps because she lost her own mother in this way. Against the rules, she regularly agreed to meet the clients, often late at night – a source of concern for our family. Her only stipulation would be that she refused to enter a pub, meeting them instead in late-night cafes.

Although Annie had rarely travelled far from the pit village of Thrybergh where she grew up, she didn't have a prejudiced bone in her body. She hugged Mia close on that first visit we made as a small family – in Annie's eyes we were all God's children, and as this was her first great-grandchild she really couldn't have loved Mia more.

Both my parents were the product of their upbringings. My dad Norman was a handsome, loving man, with a great sense of humour and fun, but strong morals and an impeccable work ethic. I remember once asking him why he went in to work even when he was sick, and he replied, 'If you don't turn up, they might decide they don't need you anymore.' His fierce, highly intelligent mother, Mavis, was an air raid warden in Kent during World War II, and stood as a Liberal MP afterwards. While the oldest brother, Uncle

Jack, was conscripted into the Air Force, his three brothers were briefly evacuated to the countryside. When Grandma Ayliffe found out they weren't attending school, however, she returned them to the family home, a substantial, attractive property with large gardens in Gravesend. Mavis ensured that throughout the war years the three youngest received enough of an education to attend university. Jack died in the war, and Uncle Alec emigrated to New Zealand to become a sheep farmer, but Mavis (always known as Grandma Ayliffe) dominated my father and his elder brother Roland until her death.

Despite her devotion to her family, Grandma Ayliffe never accepted my mum into the family because of her working-class origins. (Grandma would knowingly deplete Mum's confidence at social gatherings by introducing her as 'Barbara, the coal miner's daughter'!) In later life, when we were all still teenagers and living at home, she happily turned up to move into our house after the proceeds from the sale of her beautiful family house in Gravesend were all spent. This house had been purchased by Grandad Ayliffe, who by all accounts was a kind and mild-mannered gentleman but rather despised by Grandma Ayliffe for not being as dashing or clever as his brother, to whom she was originally engaged, and who died in World War I.

Grandma Ayliffe would spend six months with us at our family home in Oundle, near Peterborough in the Midlands, then six months with Uncle Roland and his seven children in their huge, rambling house in Cheshire. She would do everything she could to turn the respective wives against each other, but it was to no avail, as Aunty Joan and Mum had nothing but respect for each other.

Dad met Mum on a bus on a Tuesday in 1956, invited her out to a dance that Friday and proposed to her there and then, three days after they'd met! Their marriage was a long one, and while it was not always the happiest, they stuck together through the difficult years of bringing up four very different and sometimes challenging children to their final days.

Mum, Barbara Davies, was pretty and sweet-natured, and rose to the challenge of moving out of her tight-knit mining community to go first to grammar school and then to teacher training college in Lincoln. On her second date with Dad he took her to a restaurant and she recalls not knowing how to use a pepper grinder, but she quickly lost her Yorkshire accent with its flat vowels and colloquialisms, and strived to be a dutiful wife to a husband who could sometimes be intransigent and patriarchal in his attitudes.

Mum was devoted to her family but, frankly, if she could have stopped at two children – Mark, the eldest, and my big sister Ruth – and returned to her teaching career earlier, I think she would have done so. She had definitely got a bit vague about parenting when it came to my birth, in August of 1963. I was her third child – and even in my teens a rather awkward, odd-looking girl with no interest in housework or crafts because my head was constantly in a book. Five years later, Jacqueline came along, as pretty as a little doll, and the arguments between my parents about when Mum would be allowed to go back to work commenced soon afterwards. My elder sister Ruth took over some of the parenting fairly early on in my and Jacqui's lives. As we got older, I think the strain of a difficult marriage and the lack of any overt signs of affection from Dad took its toll on Mum, and I was aware of signs of depression well before she eventually succumbed to the Alzheimer's that eventually took her from us, just two months after Mia's death.

With six of us at home, trying to make ends meet was often a struggle, especially since Dad wouldn't allow Mum to go out to work until each of us reached school age. Moreover, he never changed a nappy in his life, and even four children and seven grandchildren later I'm fairly sure that would still be the case! But we were surviving for the most part on his meagre wages and he was a committed father who taught us to respect science, engineering and literature, in that order.

He had a great love of the outdoors and of flora and fauna, but for him gardening was never a fun hobby; it was a necessity. After a few years following work around the country from one engineering project to another, with us in tow, Dad bought a 1970s brick-built monolith for next to nothing in the beautiful town of Oundle in Northamptonshire. The house was clearly cheap because it was so ugly, and it had been standing empty for such a long time that the half acre of garden was completely overgrown. For us kids the grass was way over all of our heads, which seemed like the greatest fun in the world as we could hide in it for what seemed like hours. Once we'd moved in, Dad set to work taming it, and gave over half of the garden to the cultivation of vegetables, which we ate whether we liked them or not!

Mum and Dad were like a dysfunctional, irritable version of Tom and Barbara in *The Good Life*, but without the friendly neighbours. As I recall, most people seemed to give us a wide berth as locally we were considered quite odd, being overly large in number, almost self-sufficient and completely ignorant of local pursuits such as tennis or shopping for fashionable clothes, preferring instead to read one of the many books which lined almost every wall in the house, often in double rows. As a working mother, Mum didn't become part of a coffee morning or dinner party set, so we were reliant on each other for all of our entertainment and company. During this time, independently of the family, I developed a strong friendship group of my own, and a couple of friends from those days have stayed with me through the years, one making the journey from Perth – where she now lives with her Australian husband – to Byron Bay to spend time with me after Mia's death. Our upbringing instilled in us all an independence and resilience which personally helped me to survive the death of my daughter. For that I will always be grateful.

The whole family was religious and we kids were expected to attend church. St Peter's Church in Oundle was a big part of our childhoods. Even during the time when Mum and Dad were both working and too exhausted to get out of bed for Sunday's 9 am service, we dutifully headed off and performed our respective roles as choir girls and, in Mark's case, altar boy. I loved the beautiful thirteenth-century building, with its vaulted nave and massive stained-glass windows, as well as the sense of belonging it bestowed, but as I gradually lost my faith it became a source of bewildering grief. I would cry every time I set foot in the place, I think because I felt fraudulent, but also owing to a sense of loss. Eventually I stopped going at the age of fifteen. I was fairly horrified when Ruth came back from her first year of university a born-again Christian! This cemented her relationship with Mum, but left me feeling high and dry, completely abandoned by both my real mum and my surrogate mother and former ally, Ruth.

My brother Mark was widely acknowledged to be 'the clever one', but Mum couldn't ever read his handwriting, so when he received the almost unheard-of unconditional offer of a scholarship to Cambridge University she claimed she was quite shocked to discover she'd actually been harbouring a child genius. Today, I suspect that our move to Oundle, with its sprawling and expensive private school, was prompted by our parents' realisation of

Mark's academic potential. He could be educated there as a day boy, receiving all the benefits of an expensive education for the price of a grammar school uniform. Unfortunately, the different uniform singled him out in the town, and as he got older he was bullied mercilessly. Meanwhile we town girls – Ruth, Jacqui and I – had to run the gantlet of private schoolboys every single school morning, seething at their privilege and arrogance as we battled through swathes of them.

Mark became completely immersed in the scriptures at Cambridge and lived a devout life up until his death in 2020 from heart failure, despite graduating with a double first which could have bought him any amount of fame and fortune. Ruth was similarly gifted in chemistry. This made Dad very happy. However, I was arts orientated, as was Jacqui, the youngest. Since Dad absolutely forbade me to travel before I finished a degree, I took the path that was expected of me and enrolled to study English at Edinburgh University, while Jacqui went to art college.

My political education was cemented before I left school with the arrival of an unexpected group in Oundle. Five unkempt musicians in their early twenties from Barking in Essex took up residence in a ramshackle cottage with a stuffed badger in the window. It became known as Wobbling Heights. They were members of a band called Riff Raff, and mothers across the town promptly tried to lock up their daughters and throw away the keys! The lads were widely considered by the older generation to be a malign influence, and not long after their arrival a couple of shifty-looking plainclothes police officers appeared periodically in the local pubs, believed to be monitoring their supposed drug usage.

The lead singer of the band was a young Billy Bragg, who couldn't have been more averse to drugs and crime of any description.

Despite their brash humour and seemingly cavalier attitude, the lads were a hugely positive influence on my friendship group. Billy and Robert – the drummer – were widely read and even in those early days they were proving to be gifted song writers. They lived for their work, barely drank or touched cigarettes, cannabis or any illegal substances and they were endearingly honest and fun to be around.

They weren't particularly interested in me as I was still gawky and desperately shy, but Billy definitely took a great liking to Ruth. I remember him joking to me, 'Rose, since it's your sixteenth birthday, can I kiss your sister?' A year later I was dating Robert, Riff Raff's drummer. Mum received the news unsurprisingly with horror, until I brought him home to meet her and she realised he'd read a large number of the books in our prodigious collection. Over time I also witnessed my parents' attitude towards Billy change dramatically when they realised how political and articulate he was in later years.

After I left Oundle for Edinburgh University Billy came to stay for the famous Edinburgh Festival, just as his career was taking off through the all-important patronage of the DJ John Peel. My university friends were absolutely charmed by him, especially when he performed a gig with them at a local venue, and for once in my life I became cool by association. The year was 1984 and the miners' strike was coming to a head with pitched battles on the picket lines. Billy and I spent endless hours arguing through the night about politics and who was responsible for the violence. I wouldn't hear a word against the miners because of my family loyalties, whereas I suspect Billy didn't like my endless criticism of the other side because his dad was a conscript. Essentially we were both in agreement, and the arguments were more dialectic debate than serious disagreements. One day Billy came home from a gig and said, 'Rose, I've written a new song. Here, have a listen!' He grabbed a guitar and started strumming. The song, 'Like Soldiers Do' was about two people arguing: 'Our fathers were all soldiers, Should we be soldiers too . . .' and I suspected right then what he confirmed years later, that the song was written about us and our political arguments.

But things were coming to a head for him nationally and at the end of the festival we were visited by a suave London record executive who was courting Billy for a record deal – I am always proud to say he signed with Go! Discs in our kitchen.

I remember at my first university lecture, the English professor looked around the room imperiously and said, 'We here are the elite, we are the ones who read and aspire to attain knowledge through reading.' My hackles rose; I had never encountered anyone before or since with such a thirst for knowledge as Billy and Robert. Billy had one sole qualification – an O-level in English – and yet he went on to become the voice of the working class and oppressed for decades to come. From the example of Billy, Robert and Grandma Annie, I knew that an education could be acquired without ever leaving the confines of a small community.

Nevertheless, I graduated with a Masters in English and promptly hightailed it to Istanbul to work as an English teacher for three years, much to Dad's chagrin. There were many things he just couldn't see the point in, and living abroad was one of them. Hey-ho, I knew he'd always love me. I learnt to speak Turkish fairly fluently, and as a consequence it was a matter of course for me to land a job as an author on the *Rough Guide to Turkey*. Other Turkey-related publications followed, and I meandered between teaching and writing, managing to make ends meet between the two.

These adventures abroad helped to satisfy my own wanderlust, and hearing stories about my travels was definitely what prompted in Mia a desire to explore the world. I could hardly object, but I'm glad Dad never survived to realise his warnings about the dangers of travel had been ignored. At least he would never have been one to utter the phrase 'I told you so'.

I had worked as a travel writer for some years before I met Howard in the summer of 1991, in what was then a run-down suburb of South London called Crystal Palace. A teacher friend and I had started training together in a local gym, and after sessions we would go for a drink at the White Swan in Crystal Palace. It was here that Howard and I made friends and eventually started dating.

The White Swan was ostensibly an Irish pub, and attracted a number of local characters and small-time villains. Passing trade included the notorious footballer Vinnie Jones, and some of the regulars resembled the characters he had portrayed in gangster movies after his footballing career drew to a somewhat ignominious close.

Howard knew many of these locals and was treated with a great deal of respect. However, he had enrolled on an access course in preparation for entry into Westminster University to study business, and he had every intention of pursuing an education and making his family proud of him.

Although it could be characterised that I fell for him because of his bad boy past, I actually admired his grit in trying to make a new life for himself. I helped him through uni by working while he studied, and then at the end of his degree we went on a celebratory trip to Goa in India.

I was saddened to find the place was being destroyed by tourism. The rave scene was in full swing but I preferred the quieter beaches and villages, the temples and the thick jungle with macaques peeping from behind leaves. This was my first time in India and I was determined to make the most of it. I even had an excuse to go and visit a library to take some notes and pick up information leaflets for a Rough Guide writer who'd evidently had far too good a time while he was on his own research trip. It was a successful holiday, and when we arrived back home Howard and I found out that Mia had been conceived out there!

We had been trying for a baby for three years by this stage, and Mia's arrival was preceded by a miscarriage, which made me even more determined to conceive. However, family finances meant I still needed to work during my pregnancy, and I made what felt like a fairly natural move from adult education into the English department of a local prison. It was an interesting experience, not least because we were encouraged to examine the criminal records of our students. (I was often shocked to find that the most charming and apparently sweet-natured among them could have been serial rapists or complicit in murders. Only once did I sense genuine evil, and that was when I walked past a guy I didn't know without even looking at him. I was well advanced in my pregnancy and had become accustomed to the weird, salacious glances this would provoke in some inmates, but this was different. I didn't even look at the man as I walked past, but the hairs on the back of my neck stood up, like the hackles of a dog, and I was reminded of Dad saying the same thing happened to him if he heard German spoken after the war. A completely involuntary fear response.)

The first months as a family truly were a babymoon – in the original sense of the expression – the three of us wrapped up in each other and completely happy as a family unit. My university friends sought us out to spend time with Mia since they were absolutely delighted that one of us had actually given birth at last!

When Mia was ten months old, the *Rough Guide to Turkey* was due for a rewrite and I planned a couple of research trips. My dear friend and Mia's godmother, Rachel Fisher, came with me on the first trip in the role of nanny, and although it was hard work we had a wonderful time. Mia developed a lifelong taste for Mediterranean food, and was doted on by everyone we met, giggling delightedly while being passed around members of staff in a restaurant. In one rooftop establishment the waiters made a bed for her out of linen napkins, and elsewhere she was taken from us and dandled so that we could eat a meal in peace.

Another trip was with Howard. We headed for Turkey by car and took a ferry from Greece to the south. Mia was gradually being weaned onto bottled milk, which entailed finding boiling water at short notice. One day as we were walking past a tea room, I noticed the steaming urn of water on the counter.

'Please could we have some water to clean my baby's bottle?'

The tea seller, like all other traders, was delighted by my reasonably fluent Turkish and by the pretty Asian-looking baby on my hip.

'Of course, please let me help you!'

He cleaned the bottle himself, then allowed me to add the powdered milk. He gave me boiling water and an unopened bottle of sterilised cold water to make up the bottle, and took Mia from me while I made up the mix. Mia was then passed from one man to another around the tea house, and as they bounced her on their knees and exclaimed '*Maasallaah!*' at her pretty face, she gurgled and squealed her pleasure at all the attention. The bottle was whipped out of my hand, and Mia was fed while we were given a much-needed drink of tea in a cool, dark corner of the cafe.

Growing up the third child of four, and with an August birthday when all my friends seemed to be away on holiday, I can't recall having a single birthday party during my entire childhood, and I don't think I ever recall feeling that anything about me was worth celebrating anyway. I decided to rectify that as a mother so Mia's birthday was always celebrated with a party of some description.

On her first birthday, I remember being quite embarrassed by a couple of contrasting gifts Mia received. I'd mentioned that Mia needed a new coat, and Mum and Dad, with their normal parsimonious attitude to presents turned up with a sensible wool coat which from its frayed cuffs and worn collar was quite clearly second hand. Meanwhile my university friends Les and Jacqui Binet handed me their offering. It was a similar dark blue colour to the one Mum had brought, but that's where the similarity ended. It had evidently been purchased in the West End from the quality of it, and it had fur at the collar and cuffs, and an adorable Anna Karenina-style fur hat and a matching fur muff, which all made Mia look like a little princess from the Eastern Steppes. As I surveyed both coats once the other guests had left, I helpfully suggested to Mum that the second-hand coat be passed on to my niece, my brother Mark's new baby. 'You will not give a second-hand coat to Leah!'

'Hmmm . . . Oh really? Why is that, Mum? You gave Mia a second-hand coat!'

Mum faltered. 'But then it would be third hand!' she protested.

I realised what I had suspected for years – that when you are poor, gifts can often be downgraded accordingly. But Mia was never going to feel like she was second best, and from then on, I made sure I was the one who wore second-hand clothing when times were tough so she never had to.

During this period, Howard and I began arguing more and more. I had every intention of making the marriage work, and though I'd seen Mum and Dad locked in endless conflict for years, divorces were not commonplace in my family. But it was not much fun being an unhappy couple and the rows became increasingly unpleasant. Mia was far more sanguine, and if she saw one brewing she would start to perform the most heartbreaking little dances and comedy routines to try to make us laugh. This was not the parent I wanted to be.

At one point Rachel said to me that I had to leave Howard, for my sake and Mia's. I felt angry with her, and decided that because she wasn't a mother she couldn't understand why I had to stay in my relationship. The fact that I was sleeping on a futon in the living room instead of in the marital bed was absolutely normal, I told myself, and a situation I was prepared to maintain indefinitely for my child: that's what you did when you were a parent, you made sacrifices.

But one day we had a bad row and I finally woke up to where this could be going. One good friend was also a single mother, and she offered Howard a place to stay in a flat she rented out. It wasn't ideal timing, as Howard left the day before Mia's third birthday, but I remember a sense of relief when the door closed behind him – and a sense of empowerment. On reflection I could probably have used some counselling, but I refused to allow myself to feel depressed. First and foremost I was a parent, and more than anything I wanted to make a good job of that.

One of the first things I did after Howard moved out was redecorate the massive living room in our London flat. It was on the ground floor of what must have once been a handsome Georgian house in Waterloo, so the ceilings were high, and I had to do most of the work up a ladder. Three-year-old Mia ran to get a camera at one point and took a photo of me. I asked her why and she said, 'I wanted a photo of you working, Mummy!' As if I'd spent the last few years in a state of wanton idleness!

I had been paying the bills while Mia was small – after my maternity leave, I was back to teaching and travel writing while Howard completed his business degree. However, now I decided that I'd had enough of trying to make ends meet and paying nursery fees; I wanted to spend time with my daughter. I decided to earn what living I could through freelance writing, and meanwhile enjoy Mia's company.

The next couple of years were incredibly good fun, and they formed the basis of our relationship over the next two decades. I took Mia out of nursery, where I'd hated leaving her anyway, and we spent two years visiting the sights of London. I bought us a season ticket to the National History and Science museums and to London Zoo. We spent hours visiting them, as well as other museums, art galleries and London's many beautiful parks and gardens, as well as attending theatre performances all over the city. We visited the London Aquarium and the Royal Festival Hall poetry library, and rode on the London Eye twice – the first time

Mia announced she needed the toilet as we stepped into the capsule of the enormous Ferris wheel, and the second time she sidled up to a little lad, asked his age and then said loudly, 'Hmmm . . . six? Well, aren't *you* a big boy!' Cue embarrassment and avoiding eye contact for the next 20 minutes as we slowly completed a circuit in the air. Cheers, Mia!

When she was a little older we went to the Globe Theatre to see Vanessa Redgrave in *The Tempest*. We had only been able to afford £5 'groundlings' tickets – where the audience stands for the performance, as they would have in Shakespeare's day – so I put Mia on my shoulders to enable her to see better. Eventually a kind gentleman offered us his seats and he took our places in the theatre pit, so we got to enjoy the rest of the performance from a better vantage point. I was embarrassed to have taken the seat he'd paid for, but Mia loved the play: 'I liked the bit when he was banging on the table.'

'The table? Which table?'

'No not the table, Mummy. The tabor. It's a kind of drum!'

She was a lively and inquisitive little girl, and always incredibly independent: the one thing that reduced her to an absolute state of rage was being offered help to put on her clothes or shoes. She also ran away from me in the street at every opportunity and in the blink of an eye. She hated the traditional children's reins I used when she was little to keep her close to me, so in the end I'd put her on a retractable dog lead to keep her safe when we went on our jaunts – along the South Bank or to hang out in cafes on Gabriel's Wharf. (She must have had a flashback to this when she was sixteen, when out of the blue she asked me if I'd ever kept her on a dog lead when she was little. I explained why and she laughed. By this point she had been looking after friends' children for a couple of years, so she understood only too well how little children like to run away.)

I met another single mum, Sine, in a machine knitting class run by the local adult education department. While I was struggling to create acrylic squares in hideous clashing colours, my friend always turned up with the finest wools in blended earth shades out of which she created simple, serviceable garments. I soon gave up the hobby, while she quickly went on to become a well-known knitwear designer stocked by the most prestigious fashion houses, but the friendship survived and flourished.

Sine was mother of twins Francesca and Sicily. Back then, both of us were struggling financially, but she always managed to maintain high standards, which made me laugh. I remember a picnic at Hastings Beach near her mum's house. We really didn't have a proverbial pot, but Sine turned up with marinated salmon, heavenly salads, cut-glass flutes, silverware and napkins. Meanwhile the twins were dressed in linen and cashmere for a play date on the beach!

Sine and I have stayed friends and she's always welcomed me when I turn up from Derbyshire unannounced to sofa surf in central London. 'I'm sorry, darling, I have absolutely nothing in the fridge . . . Oh hang on . . . apart from this sushi and champagne if that's any good?'

Sine was a model mum to the twins, and we shared a desire to see our children thrive, so we spent many a long day together in London's parks and museums. On a recent visit to their home, Francesca described visiting us in our flat in Waterloo back when the girls were kids. 'As soon as your back was turned, we used to sneak up into your platform bed, Rosie! Mia would lie between us holding our hands. One time I told her she was holding ALL of

Sicily's fingers but only four of mine! She grabbed the other finger and I was immediately placated!'

The girls were larger than Mia even though they were a year younger, and they were far too exuberant for many of their friends, living in a kind of bubble of garrulous fun and fighting, but Mia adored them. Fran recalls being in fancy dress at our house, in a tutu, crown and spangly wings. Mia stood squarely in front of her, highly indignant at the age of six, saying, 'If you speak to your sister like that again, I'm taking that crown off your head!'

'Imagine a six-year-old putting you in your place like that!' Fran mused. 'Nobody else could control us like Mia could!'

I managed to carve out a couple of good writing roles through the *Time Out London* guides, and a friend joked that I always managed to find the perfect job for any situation I found myself in. I became a restaurant reviewer, and also a toy reviewer for Time Out's monthly parenting magazine. This was great – we received the very best and most fun toys through the post and we'd test them together and get to keep them. Every week was Christmas in our house, and Mia's friends used to love coming to visit and play. One of our favourites was an entire Playmobile jungle, and I made a papier-mâché island for Mia to display it on.

My father was a civil engineer by trade, but had a love of wood and woodworking which dated back to his childhood. When I told him about a rocking horse my Uncle Roland had made for his brood of seven children, Dad was determined to go one better. The result of his sibling rivalry was a perfect little rocking horse carved out of mahogany, complete with a saddle and bridle, and a genuine horsehair mane and tail. Dad was no mean woodworker, and I knew only too well what quality of product we were looking at. I was enormously impressed by his talent and touched by the gesture, and along with the hours he devoted to her care, it very much endeared him to Mia. In years to come, Mia showed how much she appreciated the art of present-giving by choosing just the right gift at the right moment, and I now cherish the clothing, accessories and ornaments she evidently selected with such loving care.

Back then times were hard, however, and although I tried to hide it, I was never sure how I was going to make ends meet. I remember once saying to Mia, 'I don't know how I'm going to get to the end of the month this time', and her rolling her eyes and replying, 'You say that every month, Mum!'

Dad proved how much he worried about us when he offered me my share of the family estate, which would have been enough to pay for a house of our own, as he was just about to lock up the money in long-term trust funds. It's my one lasting regret that I was too proud to take the money. It would have bought us security, and I could have been a stay-at-home mum. Instead I decided to instil Mia with the work ethic we'd all been brought up with. But today, when I'm feeling low, I ask myself, what use is a work ethic when you're dead in the ground?

Instead, we stayed in our somewhat dubious rental accommodation in the busy heart of London. Right opposite our front door was a clanking billboard that rotated to change adverts, only it was stuck forever on an advertisement for a strip joint called the Spearmint Rhino Gentlemen's Club. Every morning we were greeted with the image of a crouching woman in her underwear, staring hungrily at the camera like some big cat, and just in case we'd managed to ignore her, she was accompanied by a constant clicking noise as the page tried – and failed – to turn to the next advert. Another memorable billboard we sometimes drove past when Mia was a toddler showed a picture of the children's character Pingu holding aloft a fish skeleton. For some reason this seemed to fill her with horror, and her first full sentence was the muttered words, 'Me not eat fish like Pingu!' often repeated with a look of alarmed determination on her face.

As we drove around Central London with Mia strapped into her car seat behind me, she developed the unnerving habit of shouting 'Baby Jesus!' at the top of her voice, which more than once had me ready to slam on the brakes in anticipation of a mother crossing the road, before I realised she was making a reference to some church we were passing.

In the winter of 1998, Mum called to tell me that her dear mother Annie had passed away. This was our first loss of a family member, and I took it hard. As the tears flowed down my face, Mia proved her almost umbilical emotional connection to me and immediately burst into tears herself. 'Does that mean she's in the ground now, like William's grandma?' she sobbed. William's mum was a committed atheist, and had obviously brought her kids up without reference to God just as I had with Mia.

'No, she is not,' I said emphatically. 'She's in heaven with God and the angels, Mia. God will look after her, and when I die, I'll join her.' Children need a way of coping with death, and that was the best I had to hand. It made me realise that perhaps I should search out some spiritual guidance for Mia, despite my own agnosticism.

I started taking Mia to the local Sunday school at age three. I decided enough was enough, however, when I was called to one side and told that Mia, then eight, had been trying to convert the other children to Buddhism! This was nothing to do with me; she had discovered books on the subject at my friend Trudy's house, and Trudy had lent them out to her, touched and impressed by my daughter's fascination with the philosophy, something her own children never shared.

Mia started nursery at Walnut Tree Walk Primary School, in nearby Kennington, at the age of four and a half. I was happy to have found a school where the arts still flourished, and the head teacher refused to implement the controversial new SATs examinations in favour of a free and child-centred approach to education. Some of the children were very poor and from refugee families, but not one of them walked past you without a smile and a greeting. At the beginning, Mia attended in the mornings only, so we still had our afternoons to continue our explorations of London.

When Howard first left, Mia was desperately worried about him. I remember one day talking to her about this and having to brush away big fat tears as they rolled down her cheeks, a heartbreaking thing for a mother to witness. I asked her how she felt about her dad and she said she was worried he must be lonely living alone in a flat. As Howard's visits became more sporadic, however, she began to lose faith in him, and it was no surprise to her when during that period his visits eventually dried up altogether.

Probably because of this lack of input from her father, Mia formed a strong bond with my dad Norman, and I made sure we made frequent visits to see my parents at the family home. Mia sometimes stayed there for a few days by herself. She adored Dad, even asking if we could go and live with him once Mum was taken into a home. In his last days, when Dad was struggling for life in hospital, he found it difficult to distinguish between Ruth and me, but whenever Mia appeared in his room he would light up and call 'Mia!' in a joyous tone, holding out his hands to her in such a welcoming manner. When I told him he should think about coming to live with us in our own home he was delighted and I think it kept him alive for a few more days. Mia and I visited together as often as we could, and I was so proud of how patiently she nursed him, replacing his oxygen mask every time he pulled it off, and helping to spoonfeed him his meals. His death in 2014 was a terrible blow to us all, but Mia's acceptance helped me incredibly. Mia and I were with him as he passed and afterwards we headed to St Peter's Church in Oundle to sit together in the side chapel and pray with the minister there.

It was only at Dad's funeral, when Mia got up to read a little handwritten eulogy, that I heard about an incident that had occurred when they were together. She recounted how she'd once been out in the garden with Mum and Dad and found a dead baby bird. Mum told her to leave it alone, but Mia ignored her and went back later to pick it up and put it in her bedside cabinet. Over the following days the bird's body started to decompose and took on an appearance that frightened Mia, since maggots were starting to materialise, but she was too scared of what Mum would say if she found out Mia had disobeyed her, so Mia was paralysed. Eventually Dad had found her crying over the maggoty body, and he soothed her. Together they took the little bird outside, dug a grave and buried it, Dad promising not to mention any of this to Mum.

Mia said Dad had taught her to understand and accept death as a natural part of life and to understand a spiritual dimension to the afterlife.

Mia told the story in front of a packed congregation at St Peter's Church and I wept copiously throughout. However, she didn't shed a tear until she sat down, upon which she completely dissolved into sobs. I was so proud of her poise and determination.

Early on, I learnt that if Mia had a problem, she would try everything she could to deal with it before she would get me involved. Her solutions to problems could be a little unorthodox, not to mention alarming. One day I was called in to school by Mia's teacher.

'Mia was found carrying a bunch of keys, and we thought we should let you know,' the teacher told me.

'Oh, that's odd, why would she bring keys to school?' I replied. I remembered how, when she was a toddler, she had once crawled to a door with a set of my keys, and hammered on it in frustration to try to open it, and I wondered whether her early interest had turned into an infatuation.

'Well, the thing is, she was being teased earlier in the week by a group of children in the school yard, and she says it's happened a couple of times this week. This lunchtime she had the keys in her hand and we think she may have intended to use them as a weapon,' the teacher said.

I was surprised and a little bit horrified that a five-year-old had felt the need to take matters in hand in this manner, and I asked whether she was in trouble. Apparently the teacher on duty had gently removed the keys from her clenched fist and the school had decided to ignore the incident, so I decided to follow suit. What had become clear to all concerned was that Mia had a sense of self-preservation and would stand up for herself if required, and she never suffered from bullying or teasing to my knowledge at that school or subsequently.

I had a short-lived but successful taste of campaigning for change while Mia was at this school when it was threatened with closure. Located within easy commuting distance to the Houses of Parliament, we figured it might be in line for conversion into luxury apartments. The proposed new site for the school was on a six-lane highway, next to a petrol station.

With my friend Fiona, whose son was at the same school, I did some research. Pre-internet days this involved laborious trips to local libraries, but we found what we needed: the address of the council's pollution-monitoring laboratories. The statistics for the proposed site were horrifying, and meant the children's lungs would have been put at serious risk from high levels of hydrocarbons and particulate matter. I presented these findings at a council meeting about the school's closure, wondering aloud why I had done this research and not them. The upshot of the meeting was that we achieved a stay of execution, and Fiona and I felt like a pair of budding Erin Brockoviches. It was a good feeling to have stood up to the authorities and made a difference!

I started teaching part-time in a local college when Mia started at school full time. I enjoyed meeting a new group of people in a Preparation for Nursing English course, and I was soon offered a promotion to become a widening participation officer, working across the further education–higher education divide, on a project designed to get young people from working-class backgrounds into university.

I was at work in Waterloo in 2001 when the 9/11 attacks happened in the US. Central London became a no-fly zone, and

I wondered how I would get to Mia's school across the river if Waterloo Bridge was taken out.

Shortly afterwards, a formerly sane member of staff went into a state of near apoplexy, saying, 'They're out there laughing about it!' I asked who she meant and she hissed one word: 'Muslims!'

That was it, for me. My sister Ruth had been in Yugoslavia as it fell apart, and I knew from her accounts what could happen as a country became riven by factions.

I didn't want Mia to grow up in a city characterised by racial tension. And although this tension might be replicated in other cities across the UK, I had no intention of raising Mia in a city anyway. I wanted her to have a taste of the countryside akin to what I'd had with my sisters and brother. Plus, any attacks were likely to be targeted on the capital, I figured. Having grown up in a small town surrounded by open countryside, I was desperate to get away from the traffic and hubbub of Central London and back to a simpler way of life.

I started to job hunt in Derbyshire. We had recently been there on holiday, staying at a cottage in a beautiful spot called Hope Valley, which seemed to have everything: stunning countryside on the doorstep, train travel to nearby Sheffield for possible work, and it was much more affordable than London.

Mia was happy to move out of London, but not without her beloved friends. One lunchtime just before we moved she assembled a large group of children at the school gate, lined up with their coats on and bags packed. A couple of them were quite vulnerable, so staff were most concerned when they realised the children had intended to slip out of the gate into the streets of Central London and hitchhike up to Derbyshire to live with Mia. One understandably cross mum questioned her daughter Maddie.

'If Mia told you to jump out of the window, would you?'

'I didn't!'

'What do you mean you didn't?'

'She did ask me to jump out of the window, but I didn't!'

Mia had a captivating aura: she was never happier than when she had other people around her – children and adults – and she often stole the limelight with her good humour, sense of fun and beautiful smile. She had an integrity even as a small child, sharing her toys and always welcoming friends with open arms, and comforting others if they fell over or felt left out. She was particularly drawn to young people with disabilities and would seek out these friends to spend time with in parks and later during play time at school. Her love of life and lively imagination made her fun to be around, but she was also a listener, and even as a young child her advice was at once candid and well-measured. When we left London, a close friend and successful documentary maker told me she was devastated, not because I was going but because I was taking Mia away from her. I was in no doubt that she meant it.

2

Country Life

I MANAGED TO GET A JOB AT THE UNIVERSITY OF DERBY, AGAIN working to find routes to university for the working class. We were due to move in January 2002 but over Christmas Mia and I contracted flu, and I was so miserable and depleted I called the university and tried to back out of taking the job.

They asked me to travel up and have another look around before I changed my mind. I did this and was captivated again by the beauty of the Derbyshire hills. My new employer was right. It was to be a good move for us.

I also realised how much Mia had to learn about country living when I walked with her across an open field to explore the area we intended to settle in. As we were about to return to the road, I called Mia to me from where she was examining a mole-hill and she burst into tears because she couldn't find a path out! She was so used to concrete walkways she had no idea you could just walk across a muddy field to get out of it . . . I think she must have been worried about sinking into the mud! I realised I wanted Mia to experience all the pleasures that the natural world had to offer, just as I had as a child.

We made the move from London to Derbyshire in January, as planned. Our new house in the village of Hazelwood was everything I had hoped for. It was a cottage, but well lit and with high ceilings. It had open fireplaces and breathtaking views across the Ecclesbourne Valley. Pocket-sized gardens front and back completed its charm. Best of all for Mia, she had two bedrooms to herself, one to sleep in, and one to play in!

The silence was the most important factor for me, though. No traffic noise at all, only the quiet hum of a combine harvester on warm summer evenings. And the owls! Enchanting, sweet isolation – everything I had longed for.

I now had my first ever mortgage, which I'd achieved through taking a loan for the deposit from Mum and Dad. Unfortunately, although Mum was in the early stages of dementia, instead of forgetting this loan she became obsessed with it and mentioned it repeatedly every time we visited. Within a year the house had increased enough in value that I could remortgage, and I turned up on the doorstep at my parents with a cheque for the entire amount I owed them. I never borrowed a penny from them after that date.

One vow I'd made to myself was that I would never break a promise to Mia if I could possibly avoid it. This often made my life difficult, but never more so than on the day of our arrival in the Hazelwood cottage. The sale went through much quicker than I had expected and having made the move from a rental property to the cottage in my little Peugeot, we then stuck our bikes on the back of the car, flung a couple of suitcases in the boot and set off to stay at Sine's family gîte in France – as promised – leaving all furniture and assorted goods and chattels unpacked in the living room. Looking back I wonder why I didn't ever think before making rash promises!

Later, Mia reminded me of a couple more incidents that suggested that life was far from easy at that time. 'Do you remember when we used to go shopping in the middle of the night with coats on over our pyjamas?' I struggled to recollect why I would have done this, and then I recalled the awful electrics we had inherited, and how I had had to go out to buy fuse wire to fix a blackout. The other thing she recalled was my practice of letting the car freewheel down the hill, often backwards, in order to start the engine, because the starter motor had given up and I was waiting for my wage cheque at the end of the month to get it fixed.

I had been a little worried about how Mia would settle in at her new school. Because of her heritage, she looked slightly different to the other girls, and I wondered about the wisdom of taking a darker skinned daughter up to the Great White Hills, as southerners called Derbyshire. But stereotyping is learnt behaviour and therefore the domain of older children, and my daughter was a pretty and confident little girl who made friends quickly. Their teacher told me that Mia's dark mane of hair was the main attraction, and classmates all wanted to play with her because of it. Who can fathom the minds of six-year-old girls?

In fact, stereotyping cuts both ways. I struggled to tell Mia's friends apart as they formed a sea of Aryan features and blond hair! I was used to London primary schools, where children were from a wide variety of ethnic backgrounds.

After the move, I asked Mia whether she preferred living in London or Derbyshire, and she promptly replied, 'Derbyshire, because they look after their old people better.' I wondered what she meant, and then I realised that Waterloo, despite its slow gentrification, was still a favourite haunt of homeless people, who lived under the massive overpass and begged for money from passers-by. Mia thought they were old people who had just been left out in the street, because that's what Londoners did!

I worked hard in my new job at the University of Derby to try to feel deserving of the post. I was now running their summer school. I enjoyed the work and liaised across departments to grow the summer school provision and to increase participation. However, this meant that I was working in Mia's summer holidays, which was a logistical problem. I got around it by employing an au pair, a lovely young Polish woman who came to live with us for our second summer in Hazelwood. Mia liked Agnieszka, but she didn't like being separated from me, and for the first time I started to hear reports of Mia being irritable and difficult. Agnieszka was sleeping in Mia's bedroom at that point, while Mia had moved to the playroom, and in the style of many cramped Derbyshire cottages the two rooms interlocked, so you needed to go through one to access the other. Mia locked the door of her room one afternoon, and poor Agnieszka was left outside, unable to access her belongings.

Mia always wanted siblings, and I worked hard to make sure she had companions of her own age. An overwhelming sense of achievement hit me on the day Mia's friends came to our house to get ready for a school disco, when we had had a large fall of snow in the afternoon. The hamlet of Hazelwood is located on a steep hill above the town of Duffield, where most of Mia's friends lived, and I was getting ready to drive them down to the school when they decided unanimously that the snow took priority, so their disco leggings and crop tops were discarded in favour of a selection of my and Mia's woolly mittens, thick coats, hats and knitted scarves.

They sledged in the steepest field they could find until long after dark before heading back, exhausted, for mugs of steaming hot chocolate and butternut squash soup. It was Mia's first sleepover in Derbyshire, and they were all out for the count by 9 pm! This was the first of many such snow parties, and in years to come the girls would employ our dog, Tom, a husky–collie cross, to pull the sledges back up the hill for them. Sleepovers became the order of the day, and that crowd of blond heads started to materialise into a strong friendship group of sensible young girls from great local families.

The little house on the hill in Hazelwood had a single major drawback: it was quite remote from shops, so I was always having to nip to buy groceries after the school pickup. When Mia was eight, I felt confident enough in the local community and in her common sense to allow her to go into a grocery shop on her own and collect the provisions for the evening's meal, so I penned her a shopping list, and she happily skipped in to the shop while I waited in the car, parked on a yellow line outside.

She quickly emerged with a bag of shopping and handed me my change. 'I got the butter and pasta, Mum, but not the meat. I'm sorry but I'm not paying £3.80 for four slices of ham!'

I had to laugh, realising our tight budget had taught her to watch the pennies far too early in life! On the whole, though, I felt Mia was learning good priorities in such a safe rural community, and would thrive on a diet of fresh air, outdoor activities and good company.

Although she inherited the family passion for reading and learn-ing, as Mia grew older the continual struggle that school presented to her suggested dyslexia. She was tested at primary school and this proved a correct diagnosis, but with lots of extra help she still enjoyed learning. She also became involved in a range of other activities such as chess club, gymnastics and climbing.

These were happy years for us. We acquired our first rescue dog, one that didn't mind being left while we were at work and school because of his previous life experiences, and he proved a wonderful companion to Mia and was remembered fondly by Francesca and Sicily from their visits to Hazelwood. Mia spent the odd weekend with my mum and dad in Oundle, and with Ruth, her husband Mark and daughter Emily who had now settled down there too. Mia re-established contact with Howard and her half-sisters Tanya, Nicola and Natasha, relationships that became strong and lasting. We also discovered that Mia had a cousin called Aoife who lived in nearby Birmingham and resembled Mia very strongly. The two girls became close, and Aoife was another young person who was later devastated by Mia's death.

At secondary school, Mia had friends from many different groups. She was confident, sassy and popular, and seemed to breeze through all factions and fallouts and stay friends with everyone. She was one of those teenagers you couldn't move around a classroom to quieten down, as she just made a new friend wherever she sat.

Mia's biggest fault was one that actually sprang from her highest virtue. She had a powerful sense of right and wrong, and was incredibly protective of her friends, especially if she thought they were being bullied. However, she didn't always go about rectifying things in the right way.

When Mia was eleven and in her first year of secondary school, her friend Ellie was in an argument with a lad. When he started losing the row, he turned to Ellie and said, 'Anyway, your mum is a one-legged freak!' The mother in question had a prosthetic limb, and Ellie was mortified that he knew this, and that he had used the information to humiliate her in public. Mia, without a second thought, grabbed the lad and kicked his shins hard! She recounted the story to me later and I explained that she'd had the right impulses but absolutely the wrong solution.

At the end of that year, I heard Mia talking to some friends who had been repeatedly teased and tormented by this same lad, who sadly was really struggling and taking it out on them. I listened quietly as the girls listed some of his bullying and teasing behaviour, some of which sounded quite sexualised, and how he seemed to need to tag along with them as a group anyway. Mia told the girls they needed to freeze him out, deny him any attention until he started to behave himself better, and insisted that nobody should have any dealings with him until they could trust him. I walked away at that point. Mia had definitely learnt better ways to deal with this character over the course of the year, and I couldn't really have counselled the girls better myself. I saw Mia growing up and taking control of her environment, and this gave me more confidence in her abilities to cope with the wider world.

Mia had a love of acting and drama which meant she was often picked for lead roles in school plays, and she attended drama clubs throughout her teens. I have recently received Mia's full drama portfolio from her secondary school, from a kind administrator who was clearing out the drama department's archives. Mia's best performance by far from the selection of clips I was given was in the Willy Russell play *Blood Brothers*, that of a harangued mother of seven, forced to give up a child for adoption. As she moves across the stage looking lithe and pretty, sporting a fairly

convincing baby bump and talking about how much she adores
her brood, I am mesmerised by this vision of a future that could
have been hers.

In fact, Mia's greatest interest was childhood development. She
absolutely loved small children, and she avidly watched *Supernanny*
on TV, a program about a woman who would take over where
parents had failed to instil discipline in their offspring. Mia was
baby-obsessed from the moment she started school, always
running over to peer into prams as a little girl.

Mia started caring for my friend Jo Wiltshire's young children
from the age of fourteen. It was the summer holidays, and I'd give
her a lift up to Jo's farm in the Derbyshire hills every morning and
collect her in the afternoon. (There was always an adult close to
hand if need be.) Jo's husband, Ned, had doubted the abilities of
such a youngster before he met Mia, but he was soon won over by
her capabilities. She formed a strong bond with their two deeply
imaginative and caring children, Stan and Rowan, and really enjoyed
the challenges and rewards that childcare can bring.

When their third baby, Sonny, came along, Mia continued in a
caring role with the Wiltshires, as well as with other kids who visited the farm. She had the measure of them all, and loved them
for their differences, their incredibly lively imaginations and their
caring, compassionate natures. She'd come home after a long day
at the farm and tell me about some of the activities she engaged
the children in, the intricate treasure maps she drew or a session of
portrait painting resulting in a banner for a party. Trips into town
entailed a two-mile walk down from the hills along a leafy lane
into Wirksworth to buy ice cream. Often other parents would leave

their children at the farm for Mia to look after, although we were always careful about the legalities.

One friend told me how she would walk in on Mia at the end of a day with the kids. 'She'd be languishing on the sofa, apparently examining her nails or reading a magazine, but each one of them would be engaged in a different activity. She made it all look so effortless!'

By this stage Mia was at secondary school, and I was now teaching at a school in the north of the county in Chesterfield. I decided that we needed to move house to make her journey to school more manageable. She'd been taking two buses and in the dead of winter, standing at a bus stop in Derbyshire is no joke as the snow can drift to waist height – and buses sometimes don't turn up at all. So we upped sticks, rented Hazelwood out and found a lovely rental in the little town of Wirksworth.

There was one event in Mia's childhood that was perhaps more traumatic for me than for her. It was a summer evening of Mia's fourteenth year, and we were on the way to an open-air concert in a local park when I managed to miss the turn-off. Mia was sleeping in the back of the car, and unbeknown to me had taken her seat-belt off.

I drove some way looking for a turning place and found a lay-by. Having checked visibility both ways, I did a U-turn in the road, only I didn't quite make it round. We were stationary in the road when a car came over the horizon, but I was confident it would see us and stop.

It didn't stop. The BMW must have still been travelling at around 95 kilometres an hour when it hit us sideways with terrifying impact. According to the tyre marks, our little Peugeot was shunted some distance.

I looked around for Mia and she wasn't there! The terror I felt at that moment as I realised she'd been thrown out of the car is something I'll never forget. I found her on the grassy verge, wide-eyed, but showing surprise rather than fear. However, when she heard the panic in my voice she asked, 'Am I going to be okay?' I told her to wiggle her fingers and toes, which to my relief she promptly did.

By the time the police and ambulance arrived Mia was really perky, and managed to charm them all with her high spirits. Because she'd been thrown from the vehicle and landed on a grass verge, and because our car was so lightweight, she had got away incredibly lightly with two cracked vertebrae and a broken collarbone. The police said if she'd been wearing her seatbelt at the time, or if we'd been driving a more substantial car which had stood its ground, she probably wouldn't have survived.

Although Mia missed some weeks of schooling, she didn't sustain lasting damage. Carrying a rucksack did become somewhat painful for her, however, as well as standing for any great length of time. Nevertheless, she completed her Bronze Duke of Edinburgh Award, hiking the requisite miles with a huge backpack despite not really being a walker and having to deal with a degree of pain. I remember laughing at a text she sent me while she was out with her group on the hike. 'Mum, there's lambs in these fields!' Really? Lambs in the fields of Derbyshire? You don't say!

The effect of the accident on me was more psychological. I was deeply affected by the fact I'd nearly lost Mia, and during the following months had frequent flashbacks to the accident. I realised what she meant to me, and I became almost obsessive about being there for her for the next few years.

The first year after the accident I really couldn't cope with my job, and I only realise now that I was suffering from post-traumatic stress disorder. I would look at detailed sets of lesson plans I had written before the accident and wonder how on earth I had been able to produce such material, because I certainly wasn't capable of any analytical thought that year. I left the school as soon as I could after the children went home, and took my marking and preparation home with me. In fact, I rarely left the house other than to go to work. I gave up my much-loved hobby of climbing, too, as it took me away from Mia and I wanted to be with her as much as I could.

Four years later Mia was awarded a financial settlement because of her injuries. It wasn't enough for a deposit on a house, but was a tidy sum to pay for an extended trip abroad, so we agreed that it should be earmarked for that, and although she 'borrowed' from her travelling account now and then, she always topped the amount back up with her earnings from various part-time jobs.

Perceptive even at a young age, she became disconcerted at the amount of time I spent indoors, and the fact I had no hobbies or interests. I think she knew she would worry about me if I devoted my whole life to her, and when she flew the nest I'd have nothing.

Although Mia and I were close, this sometimes became stifling for her, and as she got older this would manifest itself as criticism. Once I told her off for not helping enough around the house, and she stormed out and went to stay with a friend. I wasn't unduly concerned as this was quite normal in our town; I'd hosted other youngsters when they were going through fraught times with their parents, and on the proviso that they let their families know where they were I would let them stay for as long as it took to let the dust settle. (On one occasion a stay lasted so long I was wondering whether to start charging rent!)

Anyway, Mia was staying with a nice family and her sulking lasted for a good 24 hours before she texted me to say, 'Mother dear, you need to understand that young people are NOT going to prioritise household chores of their own volition as we have far more pressing priorities. It is your responsibility to give me a schedule and to ensure I keep to it, rather than losing your temper after the fact.' So that was me told. Parenting squarely filed under 'needs improvement'! I'd been admonished for my lack of parenting skills fairly frequently, and only occasionally did she admit that I'd probably got it right on a couple of counts: she was happy that I'd fed her 'real food' instead of frequent processed dinners, and she also thought I'd got the balance right when it came to discipline.

Another disagreement over the dinner table saw Mia picking up a plate and throwing it at a wall. This came out of nowhere and being so out of character it surprised us both, so much so that we couldn't stop ourselves from laughing. I think in that brief moment we both saw that there was a lot of me in Mia. I regretted the laughter a few weeks later when I heard the sound of broken crockery coming from the street outside. Mia was supposedly doing the washing-up in our ground-floor kitchen, but instead of cleaning the plates she was throwing them into the street. This time we had serious words about safety, household economy and acceptable behaviour, and she took it all on board, or so I thought!

*

The following year, another of her school friends, Katy – someone she wasn't particularly close to at that point – was walking home from school with two other girls following her, calling her names and spitting in her face. They were angry over some relationship that was going on behind their backs with a lad, and had decided to see Katy off. Katy texted Mia to ask for help. The girls then happened to walk past our front door. Mia charged out and meted retribution on Katy's tormentors with her feet and fists, despite the fact they were older and much taller than her.

I spoke to a friend who lived locally and knew all the girls, to ask how he thought I should react. He said, 'Well, frankly I'd be very proud of her!'

I was conflicted, but I couldn't let Mia know that. It was not acceptable under any circumstances to resort to violence. We talked, and she listened, and this was the last incident where I heard of her fighting physically, until of course she fought her killer, and for her own life.

A few days later I encountered the girls at a party, and as they cut their eyes at me I walked over and, in front of all their friends, told them to come to my house for a chat. I made it clear that if they didn't turn up I would be going round to their houses to talk to their parents. By the time I arrived home, they were standing at the door, looking sheepish. I explained that I had had words with Mia about her behaviour, but really, two on one, pulling hair, and spitting in a girl's face? I pointed out that this was actually quite unhygienic and a means of spreading germs. I asked them what it was about, knowing full well that it was over a lad. When they replied I rolled my eyes and laughed at them. 'Look at you, you gorgeous girls! You could have any lad you wanted. Never, EVER fight with a GIRL over a LAD. Think about it, it's the lad who's in the wrong, NOT Katy. He owes you loyalty. And anyway, men just aren't worth the trouble!' The girls started laughing at this feminist rant and we parted on good terms.

Bringing Mia up as the only child, and as a single parent, I felt acutely aware of the potential issues and felt my role needed to encompass both those traditionally deemed to be those of mother *and* father. It was important for me to provide her with a moral compass, as my parents had, but also to be a companion and confidante. What I was most determined to ensure, however, was that she would never be my confidante, because I didn't think it was fair for a child to take that role. If I had a problem, I would rarely share it with Mia until I'd solved it, and then I might explain the whole scenario to her, but only if I thought I'd dealt with it well! One example was my relationship with her father, which I glossed over constantly so as not to distress Mia unduly. Eventually I did explain everything, including the reasons for our divorce, and I think she saw me in a very different light after that, because she recognised I had acted as I did for her own good. It was then that she began to truly love the peaceful nature of Derbyshire, because she understood that there was no life for us in London.

However, although I still maintain this line of parenting was probably the correct one, it came back to bite me when Mia started to do the same thing, and refused to confide in me until she'd solved a problem. It was a method of dealing with an issue that I would come to realise she was using right up until her death.

Now she was older Mia became circumspect about what she would tell me, as she knew me well enough to predict my thoughts and feelings, and how I would react to her behaviour. One of the jobs she took was in a fish and chip shop. Mia worked there for a couple of years, and then abruptly left the job. I queried why she had done this, feeling a little critical that she seemed to have given the job up for no reason. Eventually, swearing me to secrecy and in a flurry of angry tears, she admitted that one of the managers at the chip shop had taken an interest in her, and she'd found herself having to avoid his prolonged hugs and wandering hands. I was appalled, and asked why she hadn't told me. She replied, 'You would have gone down there and had it out with him, or called the police or something and I don't want to have to deal with how people would react to that!'

She then admitted that the only reason she'd taken the job and worked there for so long was that she'd damaged a lad's car in an argument over the way he'd treated one of her friends (she'd kicked the bumper), and he'd said he would go to the police if she didn't pay him for the damage (which I later learnt was a small dent and easily repairable). She'd been giving all her hard-earned cash to him because she didn't want to ask me for money, and even after she'd paid off the initial sum he'd requested he asked for more. Of course I was horrified that she hadn't felt able to tell me about this, but Mia tended to solve her problems in her own way, and explain what had happened *after* the event. It was only if she felt she couldn't solve her problems that she came to me for help, and knowing this I would always do what I could to dig her out of any hole. After her death, one of Mia's friends sent me a photograph of one of her Instagram posts from 2013 which said: 'I may argue and fight with my Momma, but she will always defend me to anyone about anything. I could call the sky red and she will have my back!' This made me laugh and cry, because I never realised she knew that.

For her sixteenth birthday Mia asked for a house party, and I decided to allow one on the understanding that friends of mine could attend and make sure all went well. Mia duly invited half the youth of the town to our place in Wirksworth, and my friends reported back afterwards. Apparently Mia looked super stressed when they arrived as people were getting drunk and she couldn't control whether any damage might be done to our meagre belongings.

By her eighteenth birthday, Mia was organising her own social life, and she decided her party would be in the cocktail bar where she worked at weekends, largely because they were letting her have it for free. Although one of Mia's friends archly asked whether I could be invited, Mia considered herself too grown up for me to be there, so I went with that, of course.

However, at 8.30 pm I received a phone call: 'Muuum . . . there's nobody here!'

'I'm sure they're on their way, but do you want me to come and make the place look a bit busier?'

'Yes please!'

I jumped into the car and headed to Monk Bar, where Mia greeted me with a grateful grin and drinks on the house. She sat with me until her friends tumbled into the bar, hugging Mia as well as they could with fists full of crazy inflatable toys and gifts.

'Love you, but you can go home now!'

'Glad to have been of service I'm sure!'

And away she skipped into adulthood . . . to fall or fly.

By the time Mia was well into her teens I'd dated a few guys on a casual basis, but I think any supposed 'significant other' worked out in the early days that if there was any competition for my time, atten-tion or resources, Mia would win hands down. I remember making it explicit to one guy, after he'd actually proposed, that all my worldly goods, such as they were, would be going to Mia. He disappeared within a few days and I realised that it wasn't ever my scintillating humour and good looks he'd been attracted to. 'The age of romance isn't dead then?' quipped a girlfriend on hearing this story.

Meanwhile the house was increasing in value, and I was always secure in the fact that any inheritance my parents left would be split squarely between me, Ruth, Jacqui and Mark. Mum and Dad lived incredibly parsimoniously, and had a habit of squirrelling small sums of money into financial schemes, which meant we would one day reap the benefits.

But the truth is, until I met Stewart I never found anyone who I thought would make a good extra in my and Mia's story, so I didn't get to the point of settling down until Mia was nearly ready to fly the nest.

When Stewart and I eventually got together, Mia was happy for me, not least because she'd managed to foist my elderly care onto some other schmuck (as she pointed out to us both whenever the opportunity arose)! Up until then her proposed retirement package was more or less summed up by the cheery comment, 'I'll let you choose your own care home, Mum!' But as an only child, I knew she felt her wings might be clipped by my future needs.

Naturally Mia viewed Stewart with a critical eye at first. To his credit he understood her reticence and tolerated her teenage moods, but he also admired her. He always said she was a leader, not a follower, and she would do well in management.

Stewart had two daughters of his own from two previous relationships. Charlotte was sixteen when we met and had moved to the Channel Islands with her mum at the age of six, and Emily was eight, and lived fairly close by, so we maintained contact with her.

Stewart was close to both girls, and his experience with parenting them plus two stepchildren helped him to understand my relationship with Mia.

Although he had left school at the earliest opportunity to escape the heavy hand of a difficult father, Stewart had done well in retail and was extremely capable at house restorations, having bought derelict properties and turned them into presentable accommodation. He was also caring, and looked after his mum and grandparents, finding them a house together when they needed help.

To me he really showed his mettle when he started to take Mia out for driving lessons as a complete beginner driver – I was in awe of his nerve! She repaid this further down the line, when Stewart managed to cut his hand badly changing a light bulb while I was at work. He was dripping blood while holding the cut together, so there was no way he could drive a car. Mia, who'd had a course with a professional instructor but only just beginning to move out of third gear, ably took control, bandaging him up and then driving him to the hospital in a town 19 kilometres away, while he gave her instructions! As she negotiated roundabouts and other town-centre hazards for the first time, both of them were somewhat terrified and exhilarated, but it definitely helped them to bond.

3

Mia's Early Travels

NOW THAT I WAS SAFELY ENSCONCED IN A RELATIONSHIP, MIA KNEW she could start thinking seriously about travel.

From her early years we'd made a few trips together on *Rough Guide* research assignments to destinations in Europe. One of my favourites was to France, just after we'd moved to Derbyshire, when we stayed in Sine's family gîte in the Haute-Vienne for a week, exploring this beautiful region and sampling its local produce. The journey there had been fraught, as we'd moved into our new house in Hazelwood the day before, but I'd promised her a holiday and I was committed to always keeping promises to Mia. So we abandoned the unpacked house, jumped into my small car with luggage and a couple of bicycles, and headed for the ferry.

While there we visited the incredible testament to the Nazi occupation of France, the village of Oradour-sur-Glane. A crumbling shell of a ruined village, it was preserved as a memorial to the French resistance by Charles de Gaulle. The accompanying documentation and film, along with some quite grisly remains, may have been stark viewing for most seven-year-olds, but Mia was absolutely fascinated by the whole experience. I think I realised then that she was a true traveller, in the sense that she was, as the Turks say, *uyanik*: she was awake and travelled with her eyes wide open, absorbing knowledge and trying to grasp the history and culture of a place. We had a lot of fun on that trip with the help of a friendly local and a fishing rod we bought for a few francs in a local super-market. Much to Mia's delight, we even managed to catch a little fish (which we then threw back in).

I also really enjoyed showing her Turkey, which we visited together a couple of times. When she was twelve, we stayed next to a beach in a tree house. (Mia had always wanted us to build one together, but we didn't have a tree big enough in our garden at Hazelwood.) It was a magical time where we walked up into the mountains to see the geothermal Chimaera at Phaselis, and visited the nearby ruins of the city of Olympos, actually just a short walk up the beach. We snorkelled in the magical azure bay, gathered a huge collection of sea-shells, and made friends with locals, including a couple who took us up into the mountains to a lovely wooden restaurant which seemed to cling to the hillside in a somewhat precarious manner.

Of course, Mia's life as a traveller started before her first birth-day, when I made the research trip to Turkey with my friend Rachel to update the *Rough Guide*. One of the many small boutique hotels we stayed in on that trip was in the resort town of Kas. One morning I had to make a call to the *Rough Guide* head office from reception, so they found out I was a travel writer and were par-ticularly attentive as a consequence. Realising that the adults could probably benefit from some baby-free time they offered to keep watch over Mia while she slept and Rachel and I went out. She had retained her baby form of sleeping soundly from feed to feed so I was confident that after putting her on the breast at 8 pm she would be out for the count for three hours or more. The staff lent us a mobile phone (a novelty to me in those days) and we only went to the restaurant two doors away for the time it took to bolt a meal, but even so I remember being quite panicky at having left Mia.

Years later, after Mia's death, I listened to Kate McCann's account of the night they lost Madeleine, and thought back to our time in Kas. At first I'd felt quite judgemental of the McCanns for their error in judgement in leaving the children for the length of time they did, but I now wonder which of us can cast the first stone? And I realise that while losing your child is one thing, living with the guilt of having taken a risk like that? It's beyond tragic and I have to admire the way the McCanns have stayed true to Madeleine and never given up on her.

We made other trips throughout Mia's childhood, some-times using a house swap organisation to travel around the UK. These were proper adventures, where we'd set off as soon as school finished on a Friday evening and head out of town, arriving in the middle of nowhere and then trying to find keys, lights and other means of survival in a strange house. It was on one of these trips when I swapped our ground-floor flat in a busy London street for a remote cottage in the beautiful Hope Valley in Derbyshire, that I started to think about moving out of London. To my mind, these people had everything: a tiny cottage in a thickly wooded valley cut deep into the Derbyshire Peak District, with a stream running past their door and a three-minute walk to the station for trains trans-porting them to work in Sheffield every twenty minutes or so.

Mia had also made trips abroad with her father, who was work-ing as a roadie for bands travelling all over Europe. She visited a number of countries: France, the Netherlands, Greece, but her favourite by far was Italy, which she fell completely in love with at first sight. She really wanted to settle there from a young age. One of the stories she came back with was that her dad was friends with Joss Stone! I asked what on earth she meant, having a hazy idea of who the famous singer was, and Mia produced a photograph of the two of them together. On another occasion she said she'd been looked after by band members of Goldfrapp while Howard had been working. It wasn't exactly the high life, but she was getting a real taste for travel and adventure.

As she grew old enough to travel independently, Mia also made trips abroad with her friends and their families, once to a villa located in the Tuscan mountains near Pisa and also to Amsterdam.

I love a story I was told about Mia in Florence when she was seventeen. She was there with some of her friends, including a girl called Lydia and her parents – Esther, a glassware designer and her husband Paul, the owner of our local cinema. Esther told me that Mia had been crossing the road and was standing at a traffic island in shorts and a crop top. As she did so she turned with one hand on her hip, perusing the traffic as she waited to cross. Traffic chaos ensued, as cars screeched to a halt and Italian motorists started honking their horns and calling to Mia! Esther was highly amused at the level of attention Mia received, which was out of proportion to anything attracted by the other girls in the party, but she did have a certain poise which singled her out even then.

From these early forays, Mia saw travelling as the ultimate adventure. She started working evenings and weekends in cafes and bars, saving money for her travels.

*

By the time Mia was nearing the end of secondary school, she was struggling. She realised it took her far longer to get anything on paper than any of her peers. It's the only time I ever saw her close to despair. She was a practical soul, outgoing, sweet natured and with great people skills, a natural on stage and fun to be around. But academic she wasn't. I felt as she did, that she needed to get out in the world and try a few different kinds of employment to establish exactly what she wanted in life. I had a feeling she would probably go to university as a mature student, which was entirely feasible, but I was happy that she had completed a childcare course to level three, which was what was required to study at university, so a gap year seemed like a suitable option.

Mia and her friends, and many of mine, talked to her endlessly about places she should visit when she travelled and what to do when she got there. Gradually a year-long trip began to take form. As she planned her itinerary she asked me about places I thought she should visit, and I think I was responsible for some of her choices. Turkey, Morocco and India were all favourites of mine.

The inclusion of Australia was never my idea. It hadn't ever been on my bucket list, probably because I knew very little about it. The word always conjured up images of red earth, vast empty spaces, ocean rollers and a carefree attitude to life. I was warned that Mia might encounter racism, and at first I was quite troubled at the idea of Mia travelling there.

However, my cousin Henry's dear Singaporean wife, Bee Lin, told me that she'd only had positive experiences in Brisbane, and the sole racist comment she'd received had been while in Melbourne. This put my mind at rest. Mia's older half-sister, Nicola, had spent a couple of years in Australia working for Qantas, and loved it so much she was struggling on her return to London. Other friends had settled there and were working in good jobs. They talked about the sun, sea and surf, but also great rates of pay and endless opportunities for young people.

So the route took shape, and Mia began organising her journey, cross-referencing endlessly with guide books lent to her by friends, and internet research. She had decided to book her tickets one by one instead of a single round-trip ticket, because she knew it was cheaper to do it like that. She planned and plotted, purchasing her visas and making sure she had all the right vaccines. I was proud of her for being so organised and together about it all. At the age of twenty, she seemed to have covered all bases, and she was good to go by late 2015.

Mia's original plan had been to travel with her cousin Aoife, until it materialised that Aoife's idea of a holiday was to stay in a five-star hotel with wheeled suitcases and preferably a boyfriend in tow, so their plan soon fell apart! Mia started to make other arrangements with her ex-boyfriend Elliot but he had already done his travelling and decided he wanted to establish a career in the music business, so solo travel became her default position, and frankly she was terrified. Much as she wanted to go on an adventure, she was leaving so much behind in terms of family and friendships that her nerves were mounting as she spent sleepless nights wondering whether she was capable of making this trip alone.

Eventually she voiced her concerns to me in a soul-searching conversation that I will never forget. She asked me whether or not I thought she could do it. I thought about it, wanting to give her an honest answer, and replied that, yes, I believed she did have the necessary skills to make a success of a big trip like this. I pointed out that she was lively and vivacious, and therefore people would want to spend time with her. I told her that travellers tended to hang out together and that she would be in demand as a companion because she was fun to be with. I reminded her that I was always there for her, and if she needed me I could help her out either financially or in person. It never occurred to me that she would be dead before I realised she was in trouble. Knowing what I now know, would I have answered differently? Of course I would, but I suspect she would have gone anyway, without my consent, and we would not have maintained the contact we did up until that awful night in Queensland.

Mia asked me what advice I would give her about travelling generally and in Muslim countries in particular, and I told her to observe how the locals behaved and to follow their customs. I pointed out that it would be best to cover her shoulders and legs when out and about, and to carry a scarf so that she could always cover her head. I told her to watch the manners of the women, and not to engage in eye contact too much with men as they might consider it flirtatious. I also advised her to make friends with other travellers, and to go about in a group, preferably with men around so she appeared to be protected.

As it turned out, her first trip, to Turkey, was almost cancelled because of a mini coup attempt in July 2016. Stewart, Mia and I watched the action unfolding on TV and it was frightening for all of us. It made me think twice about whether Mia should visit Turkey at all. As it happened, a kind of stalemate was re-established quickly – it turned out not to have been a coup so much as a minor infraction on the part of the followers of an exiled cleric – so the last-minute plan was for Mia to depart as scheduled, but to stay with friends of mine.

*

As the day for Mia's departure approached she became more and more irritable, partly I'm sure because of nerves, but also because we had recently moved into a house in the nearby village of Cromford that Stewart and I were renovating, and everything was either 1980s retro decor or covered in rubble and dust. At first she found this hilarious, and went into every room taking photos for a social media post of all the dreadful materials on the walls and floors and the hideous fixtures, including tiger- and zebra-striped carpets, clashing florals and a frankly quite disgusting bathroom suite which was the colour of rotting eggplants.

When she could make time, she helped out too, and Stewart was particularly impressed when she climbed a ladder and helped us paint the front of the house. She then asked how often this task needed to be performed.

'Once every ten years or so,' was Stewart's reply.

'Okay, could you make sure you do it again before you die then, please?'

Stewart recounted this to me later and we laughed at this typical example of my daughter's cheekiness.

There was another funny moment when she arrived home a few days after we'd moved, walked into the kitchen and started telling us in animated fashion about an incident she'd just encountered in the village. She'd witnessed a car accident, and had helped out at the scene by talking to the victims and calling the emergency services. She was incredibly proud that she'd kept her nerve and been useful, and that the family had hugged and thanked her when the ambulance arrived for an injured party. The story was fifteen minutes at least in the telling, and it was only when she paused for breath that she said, 'Oh! The wall's gone!' Stewart had knocked a partition wall down between the kitchen and dining room just minutes before she'd arrived and we were both standing on the pile of rubble.

One evening, Mia's rising fear about embarking on her journey led to irritation, culminating in her screaming at me that she hated this house and never wanted to see it again. (I think I'd probably had the temerity to ask her to pack her belongings in preparation for the redecoration we were planning when she was away.) We both took some deep breaths and I hugged her before she packed a bag and left to go and stay with her friend Ro.

I'd had a rule since she was little that we would never part on bad terms in case something happened to one of us, so I called her and suggested we meet up and go for a final meal together, which we did, just to make sure we were parting on good terms. Mia returned home two days later and together we packed the rucksack I'd purchased for her trip.

Our local railway station is incredibly picturesque and I've always found it a peaceful place to hang out while waiting for a train – especially in summer, when the lovely villa-style waiting room with its mullioned windows (featured on an Oasis album cover) is framed by meadowsweet and willowherb that provides a feeding ground for lazy bees. I had taken Mia there many times over the previous few years. In 2009, when she was fourteen, a body was found in the boot of a taxi in the charming little courtyard out front. Because of this, Mia never liked to wait there alone, so I had seen her off from the platform countless times when she made trips around the country or just to take the train into Derby for a day of shopping.

Driving her to the station this time felt a little different, because this was a long journey. But I assumed we'd see each other within the next twelve months, even if it meant Stewart and me flying out to wherever she was for an extended vacation. Little did I suspect this would be the last goodbye, the last hug, and the last time I would stand and wave a train carrying my beloved daughter into the distance.

I repeated the words I used to say to her when she was little, 'Love you all around the world and back again, baby girl!' and made her promise to stay in touch and post lots of photos on social media. And then she was gone. The last goodbye.

4

To Fall or Fly

So began for me a vicarious journey across the world. I became the ultimate Facebook stalker, watching out for Mia's every post, and messaging her most days to check whether she needed to chat.

The first stop in Istanbul was easy. It was incredibly reassuring for me to know she'd be looked after by my old friends. Ayşe and Gordon are a couple whose romance I saw develop over some years, before Ayşe built up the courage to tell her father she was dating 'an infidel'. As it turned out, Bey Gultekin was delighted to welcome Gordon into the fold (since by that stage he'd come to the conclusion that his eldest daughter must be gay), and Howard and I were delighted to attend their glamorous wedding in Istanbul.

Ayşe now worked as a senior lecturer at Istanbul University, while Gordon was the head of a language school, so they were both used to young people, and Jamie, their son, was almost exactly the same age as Mia. Both Ayşe and Gordon are incredibly kind and, as predicted, Mia had a great time hanging out with the family.

Mia was ever vigilant about parenting styles, and she always had an opinion. She could see that Ayşe adored Jamie, but sensed an overprotectiveness that she frowned on. In retrospect, I can't help but wonder whether a healthy dose of that quality would have kept my girl alive.

I could tell Mia was already hankering for the real backpacker experience, and it wasn't long before she was on her next stop in Morocco. In the beautiful photos she posted of Essaouira and Chefchaouen she had evidently taken my advice, as she was pretty well covered up and had made friends with a couple of English lads (who I duly checked out in some detail through their Facebook profiles).

Then the posts stopped.

Mia posted nothing for three days, and I went into panic mode. I messaged her on Facebook, then texted, and finally tried to ring her. Nothing.

Eventually I broke down at work and told colleagues that she was missing. One friend, a young teacher called Rebecca who was not much older than Mia, pointed out that she was probably having the best time of her trip so far, and I should stop worrying!

Eventually Mia reappeared on Facebook, looking like some kind of Saharan princess. She looked so perfectly balanced and comfortable on the back of a camel: her legs tucked under, hair swathed in a red scarf and a magical smile on her face.

She was highly apologetic as she realised from the missed messages and calls how much she had worried me, but apparently the opportunity of a trip into the Sahara, travelling by camel, had arisen and she'd jumped at it, pretty much last minute. I'm so glad now that she did, as she was exultant and had taken real pleasure from this new life experience.

The picture still brings back the flood of relief and delight whenever I see it. Mia had indeed been having the time of her life, and these experiences were all helping to build her confidence. Rebecca and other colleagues laughed when I announced her reappearance, and joked that Mia had 'just nipped to the Sahara on a camel, like you do'.

From Morocco Mia headed to India. When I'd visited Goa with Howard in 1994, I'd felt then that the tourism had an unsavoury edge to it – it was quite disregarding, if not destructive, of local culture – so I persuaded Mia to head to Kerala, which I'd heard was relatively unspoilt. Unfortunately when she arrived there she found it was raining heavily so she immediately headed north to Goa, and from there to Mumbai. I had only passed through Mumbai myself, but Mia had taken the same delight that I had in Gregory David Roberts' novel *Shantaram*, and she wrote to me excitedly about having completed the Shantaram tour of Mumbai, visiting a cafe frequented by the author.

I assumed at the time that this was an official tour, but her friend Katrina later told me the details. At Mia's suggestion, the night before the official tour, Mia and a group of Western friends decided to dress up in in traditional Indian clothing – all the women had gone out and bought saris – and they descended on a nightclub. Mia and Katrina met a famous Indian actress in the toilets who had helped them pin their saris properly. They went down so well at the club that they carried on partying until the early hours with a group of locals, and ended up sleeping in at their hostel the next day and missing the official tour, with only hours remaining before their train left town. Mia had persuaded Katrina and the others to get out of bed and accompany her to the slums on their own 'unofficial tour', apparently saying, 'You only live once!'

Katrina told me that at several points Mia disappeared from the group. Katrina would look around worriedly and find her standing in the doorway of a slum dwelling, a stranger's baby on her hip, laughing and politely refusing an invitation to dinner from the baby's mother. (I heard another story later about Mia going missing in the streets of Manchester and being found dancing with some homeless people in the early hours of the morning. My living, laughing girl, I will always admire your vivacity, your spirit and above all your ability to accept others without judgement.)

Another lovely moment for me was when Mia posted a photomontage of us she had created from a picture of me on a Norton motorbike out in Goa in 1994 (a picture I didn't even know existed, so must have been from her father's albums) next to a picture of herself in almost exactly the same pose. Predictably, she looked far more glamorous! I noticed that she had since dispensed with the long-sleeved tops and harem pants in favour of a bikini and shorts, but this was par for the course in over-touristed Goa so I couldn't really pass judgement – especially since in my picture I was wearing shorts myself.

From India, Mia flew to Thailand, also visiting Laos, Cambodia and Vietnam. Now she was more diligent with staying in touch. She visited resorts, temples and beaches, all depicted in photos in which she had generally found toddlers and babies to play with. Mia's obsession with little ones never waned. I'm sure that she would have made an incredibly fun and loving mother.

She also met and immediately bonded with a lovely girl who called herself Anna Boo on social media. The attraction was obvious as they could easily have been sisters, they were so alike in appearance and spirit. They probably spent about three weeks together when travelling in that part of the world, but they formed the kind of intense friendship that can occur while travelling.

The one major glitch in Mia's journey happened in Thailand. I had warned her that her passport would be in high demand in a country where she could so easily pass for a young Thai woman. In the event, her passport and wallet – containing her bank cards – were stolen, and she called me for help. It was at this point that we realised she hadn't set up online banking – she should have visited her bank in the UK and set up overseas online facilities before departing. This is not something I tended to think about myself, if I'm honest; in fact I've been guilty before now of doing research trips with wads of UK sterling and changing it all as I went, to avoid colossal bank fees. Thankfully Mia had good friends around her, and I put money into their accounts in preparation for the final leg of her journey, to Australia. She had also become quite ill in Thailand with gastroenteritis. A doctor gave her great advice about improving her diet, and from that point on she began to put on weight and regain her lovely curves.

After five months of travel throughout Asia, Mia arrived safe and sound in Australia jubilant at having made such an epic voyage. I too was elated that she was 'home and dry', having been on tenterhooks during some of her adventures en route. She still had the best part of her savings in her bank, and she had a job to go to, working in a canteen at Bond University on the Gold Coast, south of Brisbane.

It's an impressive campus, with marble columns and well-manicured lawns. Mia went to work with her characteristic gusto, and reported back to me that the chef had said that people didn't go to the canteen for her food anymore, but to watch Mia dance as she served them!

She made a great friend there, Misha, and they adored each other. But Mia's role as a 'dinner lady', as she described herself, didn't last long, as she found more lucrative work in a nightclub with the dubious name of The Bedroom Lounge Bar in the Gold Coast resort of Surfers Paradise.

I was mildly concerned about this turn of events. The club's social media account showed the waitresses basically dressed à la bunny girl – in a basque, stockings and suspenders. Thinking about Mia's future life and her CV, I really didn't approve.

In the end she called me to calm me down. She told me her job was serving at tables, flirting with the customers and persuading them to stick around and drink more, all of which she was good at and so enjoyed. The bedroom-style layout of the place was a gimmick, to give it a sexy sell in competition with a neighbouring club, but Mia said she felt safe working there because it was so well managed. If any of the waitresses made a complaint about a customer, they were believed without question and the said customer would be unceremoniously turfed out.

Mia lived a stone's throw away in a lovely apartment she shared with a girlfriend, Jordyn, who also worked at the club. The flat had beautiful sea views of a stretch of coast occasionally frequented by migrating whales. They also managed to smuggle a kitten in to the apartment, and Mia's phone was full of pictures and little videos she made of Leo, which she showed me over Messenger. He was very similar to Mia in character: naughty, playful and adventurous.

Mia posted pictures of herself on outings with new friends, and she did a virtual 'tour' with me of her new flat on FaceTime, showing me the views from the balcony and her bedroom, which appeared pretty well pristine compared to how she'd lived when she was at home in the UK. (I was subsequently told that Mia's bedroom frequently deteriorated into the chaos I was used to!) I could tell she was excited and happy, and enjoying life. At one point she asked me what I thought about her moving to Melbourne and attempting to broaden her horizons and gain more meaningful and career-orientated work, or whether I thought she should stay where she was with her new friends and just enjoy her time in Australia. She eventually decided to stay, a choice I'm glad she made in hindsight, as it meant she spent her final weeks with people she loved.

Four months into her time on the Gold Coast, Mia knew that if she was to continue living in Australia a second year she had a hurdle to cross, which was completing 88 days of farm work. I vaguely remembered her mentioning this before she left for Australia. I couldn't see any problem with Mia going into farming on a government program, and I envisaged something like the USA's gap year program, Camp America: well-regulated and, at its best, mutually beneficial for all participants. I envisaged Mia engaging in some hard graft, but in a team of happy backpackers, enjoying the sunshine and seeing another side of Australia. I assumed too that she would be kept safe through close supervision, with spartan but comfortable accommodation possibly part of the package, and everyone regulated for drug abuse and alcohol use.

Mia saw it differently, however, because she'd done her homework. She didn't tell me anything, but later I found out she knew about some of the perils of the 88 days, and for this reason was doing her best to get out of it. Then, just before she was due to head to Townsville to commence her 88 days she messaged me excitedly about a job prospect in Italy. A modelling agency had responded to an inquiry she'd made, saying they wanted her to work for them and were offering to fly her to Milan! For once I was keen for her to go down this route.

From turning heads in Milan to being selected for local stints of catwalk modelling, Mia had a beauty I could only wonder at. She had put on weight since arriving in Australia, as she couldn't resist the huge variety of good food available. Being Mia, this only enhanced her figure, and she now had curves in all the right places. A mutual friend, a local yoga teacher and another very beautiful woman, had once said to me, 'You think Mia's beauty is a blessing, don't you? I have to tell you it isn't – it's a curse. If you're beautiful, women want to be you, and they can't, so they hate you, and men want to have you and they can't, so they hate you too.'

To me, it seemed Mia had always had enough personality to gain friends, often in spite of her looks, but I'd never wanted her to work as a model, as I felt it was a cruel and superficial business, and really quite a boring job. However, this could be a way around the farm work, which I could see she didn't want to do. It could also bring her closer to home.

The guy who had contacted her claimed to be a director at a prestigious talent management firm. We checked his LinkedIn profile, and it all appeared to be genuine, and the email looked official.

But our suspicions were piqued when on the agency's website we read they never offer Skype interviews. If we hadn't checked thoroughly, and if she hadn't been able to run the whole thing past a photographer friend in Brisbane, Mia may have fallen into a trap which could easily lure a vulnerable traveller to take international flights into the hands of unscrupulous people. We weighed up the information we could find, and Mia messaged me resignedly saying, 'Farm work it is then!'

5

88 Days and Counting

AUSTRALIA'S 88 DAYS OF FARM-WORK SCHEME WAS DREAMT UP IN 2005 to plug a gap in the workforce of the country's agricultural industry. In order for backpackers from more than twenty countries around the world to stay a second year in Australia, they need to do a total of three months of work in agriculture, mining or fisheries during their first year, and back in 2016, paperwork was signed off by the employer. The federal government issues the second visa, but they have little to do with the program itself. The young people must find the work independently, and try to distinguish between genuine employers and the many charlatans, gangmasters and downright abusers who are attracted by their youth, vulnerability and naivety.

The scheme is important to the Australian economy: the National Farmers' Federation estimates that 417 visa holders (that's people holding Working Holiday Visa Subclass 417) comprise 25 to 35 per cent of the agricultural workforce in Australia. But why is such an important figure an estimate?

It took several months for the truth to dawn on me: there is no formal registration system for the 417 visa holders undertaking agricultural work, so nobody knows who or where they are, how they are being served by the system or how many there are. It is only after workers have received evidence of their labour from the employer, in the form of payslips, that they send their details to the government for a second-year visa to be issued. Worse: nobody knows the number of fatalities or injuries incurred as a result of their work, although I was informed by an Australian lawyer who is solely concerned with migrant farmworkers that the estimate is unexpectedly high, and that youngsters are largely unaware of their rights in the event of an injury.

Mia didn't share her concerns with me about the 88 days. She'd already determined not to travel alone to a farming environment, or work for anyone who was trying to recruit only women. For this reason she turned down a job in Caboolture, north of Brisbane, and headed instead to Home Hill Backpackers with a friend, Chris Porter, who also needed to tick off his 88 days. She and Chris arrived at Home Hill on 19 August 2016. The two of them were placed in a room with a French man called Smail Ayad. The cleaner/assistant manager Ms Weaver later deposed to the coroner that on the day Mia and Chris were due to arrive she had had a conversation with Ayad and he told her: 'Don't put them in my room, put them in Lance's room.'

Ms Weaver deposed that she raised Ayad's request with Mr Scholz (the night manager) who informed her that it would not be Ayad's choice and guests should otherwise accept their room allocations.

The evening she arrived, Mia showed me around the hostel on Messenger via a series of photos. She was right, it did resemble a prison in some respects, although the travellers probably had less space to store their belongings. Mia was evidently uneasy about the place and disliked the strict rules. What she didn't send me was a picture of the sign in the kitchen which proclaimed in large letters, 'Thieving cunts will be prosecuted.' However, she did tell me that she'd been told off in no uncertain terms for putting a bottle of beer on a shelf over her bunk. She'd been given work immediately when she arrived, and had been given the beer by her employer as a well done and thank you. Mia had an intolerance of alcohol so she drank very little and, besides, she didn't like lager, so she'd put it on the shelf to keep it out of the way. I could tell that she was shocked to the core when she was berated for bringing in alcohol not purchased from the hostel's own bar. The unfairness of it confused and upset her. It seemed over the top to me too, but at the time I assumed the place had a no alcohol policy. I later realised they were simply protecting their profits.

Mia was worried about being unable to tick off her 88 days – she had only four months left to complete them in, so she desperately needed the work. It seemed that new arrivals were being given a few days' work, while their predecessors were told by the contractors that they were too meticulous, or too slow, or too untidy. Yet the farmers were equally confused about the sudden replacement. It was all about filling the hostel to maximum capacity and maximising productivity by keeping everyone anxious and on their toes, especially those with very little time left to complete their 88 days.

This meant Mia was worried that she might be pitted against the other backpackers, and so she felt there was little opportunity for her to build friendships and enjoy her new environment. In fact, Mia didn't have a competitive bone in her body, and I regret now encouraging her to vie for work in order to finish her days. I think it's the only time I tried to persuade her to go against her nature. I'd always trusted her judgement with regard to interpersonal relationships; it was her greatest strength.

Mia's posts on Facebook made me laugh as she started to count down her days. Her first job was to pick up stones and rocks in a sugarcane field. I was startled at this – it sounded like chain gang hard labour! – but the job was widely considered to be the easiest. I had to wonder what the others were doing.

She didn't tell me much about the farm, but she did post about having seen spiders and a dead snake in the field. I shared her post, and an old school friend of mine who has settled in Australia said that Mia could expect to encounter venomous snakes in the cane fields of North Queensland. My friend said that the recognised procedure was to back off from the snake, avoiding sudden movements, and that there should be a first aid kit to hand with a pressure bandage. I asked Mia what advice she had been given regarding snakes and spiders, and she replied none at all. She'd had no induction whatsoever about how to carry out her role on the farm – nothing at all about sun safety, staying hydrated, potential hazards or dangerous fauna. She also said that she had to work fast as the harvester always seemed to be closing in on her.

I started to get curious about the whole 88 day scheme from a number of things Mia mentioned when I questioned her, and did an internet search. It was then I saw a review referring to the town as 'Hell Hill' and to 'avoid at all costs'.

I knew Mia and could read her tone of voice, and I was on red alert, feeling there was something terribly wrong. I had sensed Mia's initial unease and growing dislike of the place, and I realised this was not just a dislike of hard manual labour. Having missed a call from Mia on her third day there, I went into a state of high anxiety. When I finally spoke to her I was incredibly relieved and told her so. I asked her to write a blog as evidence of what was happening to her – I wanted her to collate data, because it seemed to me that someone could be hurt.

Mia told me that a young woman who was staying in the hostel was being treated very well because she'd had an accident. I wondered if such friendly treatment from people who evidently inspired antipathy from backpackers generally may be an attempt to placate someone who could potentially have a claim against one of the farms. To me this was more worrying evidence that things were not as they should be, especially given the lack of induction for young people who would have no idea what to expect in a British cornfield, let alone in a completely alien environment in a country renowned for its dangerous wildlife.

I knew Mia was in trouble, but I had no real idea of what the threat actually was. Less than twelve hours later she was dead.

6

Mia's Death

NOTHING PREPARES YOU FOR NEWS AS CALAMITOUS AS THAT WE received on the evening of 23 August 2016. When the two police officers told us that Mia had been fatally wounded we were given very few details. But I remember feeling a sense of deja vu, almost as if I'd known this was going to happen.

The policemen informed Stewart and me that they could give us no more information than the basic fact of her death, and we were told we needed to call the Foreign and Commonwealth Office on a number they provided us. This seemed like a strange procedure, but we were in no position to ask questions. So I called immediately, and the phone was answered just as quickly by a confident, well-modulated voice. He informed me that Mia had received her fatal wound at the hands of a young man at the hostel, a French national called Smail Ayad. He told me that there was no doubt about this as it had been captured on CCTV footage. He told me that Ayad had been heard by other backpackers to shout

'*Allahu Akbar*' as he killed Mia, and that this was therefore being treated as a possible terrorist attack. He also informed me that another man called Tom Jackson had tried to save her life, and his life was now hanging in the balance. None of it made sense; my brain just refused to believe it was true.

The policemen sitting in my living room were obviously aware of this information already. They looked devastated on our behalf; I thought they had really drawn the short straw to be delivering this news from a police station as regional as ours, where more frequent crimes were badger baiting and the occasional incident of shoplifting. As they left they assured us that Howard, Mia's father, was receiving a visit from the police simultaneously, so I didn't need to speak to anyone until the following day.

Since then, I have been asked over and over how I felt on receiving that news. The absolute truth is I felt nothing. It was like I disassociated from my emotions, as if I were a bad actor in a movie I didn't want any part of. I've learnt now about coping strategies and grief, about how the mind goes into denial, but at that point I was watching myself and wondering what was wrong with me.

I decided to call Home Hill Backpackers to try to find out more about the incident, feeling only compassion for the poor people who'd had to live through this incident on their premises. Apart from what I'd found out about the hostel online, I really knew very little about the place and I didn't want to jump to any conclusions. However, even in a time of such high emotion, I found it strange that the person on the end of the phone was at pains to tell me what a lovely man Smail Ayad, Mia's killer, had been. She said the attack had come out of the blue. I had just asked for information, and was certainly not looking to lay blame. In fact my first thoughts had been that this could have happened anywhere so this seemed odd to me.

Stewart decided to take a day off work and stay with me the following day, which was a huge relief. I managed to persuade him to take himself up to bed once the policemen had left, though, as I felt I needed to be alone and work through my emotions. We'd asked the police if there was likely to be any press interest in the story, and they said yes, probably, because it was being investigated as a terrorist attack. I figured the local paper and BBC Central, our local TV station, would arrive on the doorstep, and so I tried – to no avail – to get Mia's Facebook profile closed down. I suspected it would be pillaged for photos. Before she left the UK this wouldn't have been a problem as she was careful about what she put on Facebook, but the youth culture on the Gold Coast is very different to that of a small-town environment, and there were many photos of Mia in her night-club outfit and in beachwear. I hadn't tried to control this when she was enjoying her life, as the last thing I wanted was for her to feel I was being judgemental. She was a beautiful girl, and how she chose to dress was her business. But that night I was afraid she could be exploited for her looks in a world where people can so easily be commodified – to some extent she could still be naive and vulnerable, despite her adult appearance – and right now I didn't want the press using those photos.

The first person I informed of Mia's death was her ex-boyfriend, Elliot, who I saw was still online around midnight. I messaged him to tell him what had happened because I didn't want him to find out from the press. Mia had been involved with him before she went to Australia, and I'd hoped it might pick up again on her return. Elliot was a sensitive, talented musician, who was well travelled and had a good work ethic, and I knew he adored Mia. He was clearly devastated by the news. Later he told me that he had been about to log off and turn in when I messaged him, but he was glad he had heard the news from me rather than from the media. It also meant he could approach me to talk about his grief later, and this formed a bond between us which helped us both through the coming weeks and months.

By about 3 am UK time, the news was breaking in Australia. This became my first of many long vigils spent conversing with people on the other side of the world at what were strange hours for me in my quiet corner of Derbyshire. I spoke to two of Mia's girlfriends from the club in Surfers Paradise, Jesse Tawhi and Jordyn. They were both in shock, and I was aware of how hard it was for them to lose someone they had become so close to. They were expecting Mia to return in a few months, and had made space in their lives to receive her. Now that space was full of grief. I did what I could from such a distance to help them process their emotions, but I felt inadequate, and I really just wanted to hug them both.

I remember stepping outside to greet a pink-tinged, serene morning – it must have been about 6 am. I was in a dreamlike state from shock and sleeplessness, and my legs seemed to buckle under me. Nothing seemed to function properly, it was as if I'd been crippled by grief in the space of eight hours.

A little later, when I felt a bit more myself again, I took a coffee up to Stewart and as I opened the curtains I noticed people gathered out the front of the house, with more further down the road next to a van with what looked like recording equipment in their hands. I recognised the logo of ITV, one of our major independent TV channels, and groaned, sweeping the curtains closed as I did so. What looked like a large posse of press had arrived and it wasn't yet 8 am.

I needed to think this through, and fast. News would be out in the UK that morning, if it wasn't already, and I needed to let people know before that happened. I wrote a long post on social media for friends and family, knowing that word would spread around our small town in no time. I asked people not to speak to the press. At that stage, nobody really knew whether it was a terrorist attack or not, but it didn't appear that way to me, and I didn't want Mia's death to be used to fuel any racist or anti-Islamic narrative. She would have felt completely let down by that.

Not everyone would be on social media at that time in the morning, of course. I learnt later that my dear friend Rachel, Mia's godmother, who had travelled with us to Turkey on our first trip, heard the news on her car radio as she was driving and narrowly missed crashing into another vehicle as she was blinded by tears. Luckily she had managed to pull over before she broke down into a sobbing fit.

The Wiltshires, the family who lived on the hill farm above our town and whose kids Mia had minded for eight years, were on holiday in Portugal with Ned's brother, Tom. The whole family were apparently sitting around in the living room when Tom opened his laptop and saw a picture of Mia and an article about her death. He cried out in shock, and his wife Paula ran over to read the article. Paula broke down at that point, and poor Jo, the beautiful mother who had been a huge influence on both me and Mia, had to cope with this terrible moment. She was faced with her children's grief, her own emotions, Paula's reaction, and all on top of recent news that her own mother had just had a stroke.

What followed back in Derbyshire was the most surreal day of my life. The police liaison officers arrived first. They were very sensitive, but they told Stewart and me they were learning that Mia had died in a horrific manner. This was tough to hear. They didn't give details, but they did say they were convinced she wouldn't have felt pain because of the incredible amount of adrenaline that would have been coursing through her body in the moments running up to her death. They told us that Ayad was a French national of Libyan descent, and that we should take information from them rather than the press. They also asked me to contact their press officer when I was ready to talk to the public.

After the police left, the street started to fill up even more with vehicles, and I realised I was going through one of those nightmare scenarios you think are the preserve of others, never you. The phone rang, and journalist after journalist found ways throughout the day to ask for interviews – there was no way I was entering into a dialogue with a single one of them that day. Family members were starting to learn of what had happened, and I took calls from my brother Mark, a devastated cousin Henry in Singapore, and my two sisters, Ruth and Jacqui. Thankfully, my father hadn't lived to hear the news about the loss of his first and favourite grandchild, and Mum's Alzheimer's was at such a point that she had no comprehension of what had happened. However, I felt keenly the absence of my parents at a time when I desperately needed people to lean on.

One news reporter called to ask for an interview and a photo of Mia. I refused, and she said, 'If you give us an interview, you can say it in your own words. Otherwise, we'll write what we want to write, and use whichever pictures we want as well.' Well, that was it as far as I was concerned; there was no way I was giving in to emotional blackmail, even when I was in such a vulnerable state.

Two local friends had offered to come over, and one of them happened to own a Subaru with blacked-out windows. I gave them both strict instructions not to speak to the press and persuaded them to park the car in a neighbouring carwash. Instead of going out through the front entrance of our house, we went to the end of our garden and with some difficulty managed to climb over the fence to meet my friends.

I needed to stave off the glare of publicity for a while until I'd collected my thoughts. I felt like quarry chased by a pack of hounds, but when we made it to the safety of the Subaru I was glad that we'd outwitted them. Not only had I not asked for this intrusion which felt totally inappropriate, but also, with my world spinning into a new orbit, I felt a strong need to take control of at least this little part of it.

From there we headed downhill in the car to our local pub, The Boat Inn, in Cromford. Everyone we encountered there had heard by then, and the family who owned the pub were struggling with the news themselves as they'd been close to Mia. There were many hugs and tears.

While at the pub, I took a second call from my brother Mark who said that my nieces were being harassed by the press at their respective university campus and school, so he asked me to make a statement. I knew I was in no fit state to do this, so I asked others to contribute their ideas and we cobbled together something which I gave to Stewart, who headed back up to the house with it.

I thought Stewart would be able to pass the piece of paper with our statement on it to the journalists and then disappear, but I'd forgotten that the TV cameras were there, and he had to try to read it out. He was in a state of deep grief and near exhaustion, and consequently he sobbed through the entire rendition. If anything demonstrated the sheer horror of our day, it was his delivery. I remembered afterwards that I'd promised to make this statement through the police liaison officers, and they weren't pleased that we'd circumvented them, but that was the least of my problems.

My view now is that the press should unilaterally allow those who are grieving a 24-hour moratorium to collect their thoughts and compose themselves. One's dignity is so important after suffering a loss of this magnitude.

Later that day my sister Ruth arrived. She was upset as she'd been close to Mia. We talked through the facts of her death, and I told her that the only way I could cope was to think of Mia's death as fated. Although she was a Christian, she disagreed with me on that front. She thought that Mia's death had been avoidable.

All the time I was wondering why I still felt nothing. I hadn't cried, I felt no grief. And yet my only daughter, my darling girl, my whole reason for being for the last twenty-one years since her conception, had gone.

That evening I started to recognise that I was in denial, as when I opened up the laptop, my first instinct was to look for a message from Mia. I realised I just hadn't accepted her death. I could still hear her laugh, the one that gurgled up from her belly and spilled

out like a rush of bubbles. I even knew what her reaction would
be in such a situation. She would have been outside, with a tray
of coffee mugs, courting the press, making jokes and enjoying the
limelight. I imagined her penning a statement, eulogising herself
into a saint and adding in some sly swipes about my poor parenting!

It wasn't that I didn't know she was dead, or that I didn't know
she wouldn't come home, but it was a truth of such earth-shattering
magnitude that I couldn't accept it. In my heart of hearts, she was
still out there, and this nightmare was a trial run for reality. My
daughter wasn't dead, I could save her, surely, through sheer will-
power. The truth took a very long time to sink in, but at that stage
I was protected by my hubris, or optimism, or denial. Call it what
you will, I just wouldn't accept the loss of Mia as the truth.

7

Tributes

WE MADE PLANS TO TRAVEL OUT TO AUSTRALIA AS SOON AS MIA'S body was released for burial by the Queensland Police Service, which in the event only took a couple of days. It was decided that Stewart and I would travel out with Howard, Nicola and Natasha, two of Mia's half-sisters (the eldest, Tanya, was concerned about exposing her two children to such levels of grief given how close they'd been to Mia), and Ruby, Howard's mum.

I have always had a huge amount of respect for Ruby. She is Jamaican-Chinese, but had moved to the UK on leaving the Caribbean and worked as a paediatric nurse. When Howard was sixteen she moved to Florida where she gradually worked her way up to become the head of a paediatric unit, and even had her own house built on the prestigious Florida Keys. She is principled and spiritual, and looks after herself, body and soul, with a strict diet of vegan food and meditation. She is also incredibly kind and generous. Mia had visited her in Florida and had a wonderful time.

She had managed to persuade Howard to follow in her footsteps and live a more spiritual life, which could only have benefited him, so his girls were generally accepting of this, although some rules struck me as odd, such as the way their religion forbade Ruby and Howard to hug anyone outside of their circle.

Among all the cards, flowers and messages of love and support we received at this time, one of many acts of kindness stands out in my memory. When we finally received the go-ahead to leave for Australia I realised some of the clothing we wanted to take needed washing. I put everything through the machine on a fast cycle but everything was then too damp to pack as our drier had recently given up the ghost. Stewart asked some neighbours we barely knew whether they had a dryer and they immediately came over to pick up our damp laundry. We waited a couple of hours, wondering where our clothes were as we needed to pack, and then husband Neil turned up on the doorstep with the entire pile which had been meticulously ironed! When we returned from Australia a few weeks later, we found they'd left a meal for two with wine on the doorstep. Good neighbours are a rare and wonderful thing in times of hardship, and this family are up there among the very best.

Stewart and I travelled down to London and stayed with a friend, Juliet, and her partner, who was a TV cameraman working mainly for Channel 4 News.

That night, Stewart, Juliet and I met Howard and family, both for a meal and to plan Mia's UK memorial service. By a trick of fate we ended up in the very spot where it all started. Westow House in Crystal Palace is now an upmarket wine bar, but back in the 80s it was the White Swan, that shady and insalubrious public house where I met Mia's father. Now I was back, twenty-plus years later, putting the final touches to the plans for my daughter's funeral.

We decided the service should reflect a range of faiths without realising what we were taking on. Mia was essentially Buddhist in outlook: she derived immense comfort from meditation, and she believed in reincarnation and other tenets of Buddhism. We opted for a prolonged, reverberating note from a Buddhist singing bowl to signify the beginning and end of a meditation on life and death.

Most of the family is Christian and the memorial service was taking place in a church, so we chose Chapter 21 from Revelations for my brother to read. However, verse eight was something of a challenge: 'But the fearful, and unbelieving, and the abominable, and murderers, and whoremongers, and sorcerers, and idolaters, and all liars, shall have their part in the lake which burneth with fire and brimstone: which is the second death.' I pointed out that this included a fair proportion of the congregation. We decided to leave that bit out.

I came to the conclusion that I had no option but to read the eulogy myself, although I knew I would struggle desperately. Mia had reduced many of us to tears just eighteen months previously by reading a piece she wrote about my dad at his memorial service, and I felt if she could do it then, so could I now.

Before we departed for London, Stewart and I had spoken to Reverend Canon David Truby, the minister who would be conducting the service in Wirksworth. After talking about the mis-representation of Mia's death in the media as an act of terrorism on the part of an Islamic fundamentalist, David suggested we include a Koranic reading, and he promised to find something suitable with a friend who was an Islamic scholar. This would be delivered by Jamie, son of Ayşe and Gordon, who was planning to fly to the UK from

Istanbul for the service. We also asked my friend Mark Glanville, an opera singer of Jewish descent, to deliver a Jewish text or song.

To reflect Mia's love of music we asked Elliot to sing in church. The song which immediately sprang to his mind was about obsessive love, which was a little jarring given we were still finding out the circumstances of her death. But Elliot learnt the song with Mia at his side and it had strong associations of her to him. Nan Ruby loved the song too, so it was in, and Elliot said he would amend the lyrics to avoid negative connotations.

The flight to Australia the next day was probably the first time I really came to terms with what was happening. Seated beside Stewart, I wept for most of the journey. He was a comforting presence and shed tears himself, partly in grief, but also out of sadness to see me so distraught. The images of that terrible night – Mia's death and Tom Jackson's heroic act – played repeatedly in my mind. I was told by the police that Mia was unconscious after the first blow, but my brain refused to believe that, and instead it played and replayed the ugly scene for me until my whole being seemed to swell up with grief. I was deeply concerned about Tom's condition and whether he would pull through. I hoped to be able to reach out to his family at some point while I was in Australia.

I was also fearful of what the days to come had in store. We'd had news from Australia via Nicola (who had become PR person and PA for the entire family, and an absolute rock) that we were going to have three police cars escorting us from Brisbane airport to the Hilton to avoid the press. Given I'd already had to climb over an eight-foot fence in our back garden to get to the pub that week, I was apprehensive.

From left to right: Mark, Ruth holding Jacqueline, and me. Ruth took over some of the parenting role fairly early on in my and Jacqui's lives.

Here I'm around eight years old. I always felt growing up that I was a rather awkward, odd-looking girl.

A rare happy photo of my parents. Mum and Dad were like a dysfunctional, irritable version of Tom and Barbara in *The Good Life*.

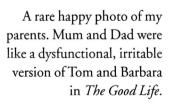

Here I'm a young student at Edinburgh University in 1984. My friends and I would have passionate discussions about the miners' strike and debate who was responsible for the violence. In the foreground of this photo, with his back to the camera, is singer Billy Bragg with whom I'd argue through the night about politics. He ended up writing a song about our arguments that summer!

This is my Grandma Annie Davies holding Mia (wearing the sweater Mum knitted for her), with Mum on the left of the picture and me on the right.

When Mia was ten months old, the *Rough Guide to Turkey* was due for a rewrite and I took her on a couple of research trips. Mia developed a lifelong taste for Mediterranean food, and was doted on by everyone we met, giggling delightedly while being passed around members of staff in a restaurant.

I can't recall having a single birthday party during my entire childhood, and I don't think I ever recall feeling that anything about me was worth celebrating anyway. I decided to rectify that as a mother, so Mia's birthday was always celebrated with a party of some description.

Mia and I were always close. When she was little I wanted to spend as much time with her as possible so I took her out of nursery and we spent two years visiting the sites of London. In recent years countless people have told me how alike Mia and I were in mannerism and behaviour. I don't think either of us realised this about ourselves.

Mia adored my dad. In his last days, when Dad was struggling for life in hospital, whenever Mia appeared in his room he would light up and call 'Mia!' in a joyous tone, holding out his hands to her.

I became the ultimate Facebook stalker when Mia set off on her journey across the world. But in Morocco her posts suddenly stopped and I went into panic mode. Eventually Mia reappeared, looking like some kind of Saharan princess. Apparently the opportunity of a trip into the Sahara, travelling by camel, had arisen and she'd jumped at it. I'm so glad now that she did.

As a young woman I travelled the globe too, living in Turkey and visiting India and Morocco. Mia and I shared the same spirit of adventure.

I was very relieved when Mia got to Australia and moved into a lovely apartment on the Gold Coast with a friend she made. She even managed to smuggle a kitten into the apartment!

Mia knew that if she was to stay in Australia a second year she had to complete 88 days of farm work. I couldn't see any problem with her going into farming on a government program, and envisaged Mia working in the sunshine and seeing another side of Australia. Mia saw it differently, however, because she'd done her homework. She didn't tell me anything, but later I found out she knew about some of the perils of the 88 days, and for this reason was doing her best to get out of it.

Nothing prepares you for news as calamitous as that we received on the evening of 23 August 2016. After Mia's death I threw myself into investigating the 88 day rule. This photograph was taken by the *Daily Mail* for an article they wrote, which led to my acquiring a profile as a campaigner. *Photograph courtesy of Koray Erol, Caters News Agency*

I married Stewart on a perfect day in November. Before the official ceremony, a number of friends and I walked uphill in a kind of procession to a memorial bench we had built for Mia. Denise, a close friend, blessed us in a very moving personalised service. It felt so right to have the wedding blessed in the hills where Mia had spent so much time.

Wedding photos courtesy of Corinne Hills

The wedding ceremony itself was packed with family and friends, and the feeling of goodwill was palpable. I think the general consensus was that we'd earned some happiness.

Many people have commented on how proud Mia would have been to see the campaign, the website and the media work I've carried out in her name. She had a sense of outrage, shared by youth generally, for anything she considered to be unfair or unjust, and she had a kindness and wisdom well beyond her years.

In addition, I knew people in Australia and at home were confused, distressed and angry about Mia's death and looking to blame someone. If I appeared to deny them the right to retreat into xenophobia and hatred, would they turn on me? Would the press start to dig about or make up things to hurt me? Who knew? I didn't care as long as they didn't discredit my girl. The thought of that brought back the fits of sobbing.

The journey gave me time for reflection. What did I choose to believe now the worst possible thing had happened? I believed that I needed to go on, first and foremost for Mia's sake, but also for the sake of others around me, particularly for my lovely partner Stewart who deserved so much more than this. He'd already carried five coffins, and one of those contained his only brother who had died by suicide.

I also believed Mia was with me on that journey. I believed we would hold each other again one day, and that the many who were grieving for her at this time would be with her again too. We would be reunited, sooner or later, in our own bright places full of love.

Messages of support and tributes were pouring in from friends and colleagues. There was a beautiful email from a friend I had known many years ago. After a gap in their contact, he described seeing Mia again at my fiftieth birthday party:

I remember being astonished when I saw Mia. She was so impossibly glamorous, like a girl out of a Bond film. And yet clearly so down-to-earth. And so like you in lots of little ways. I remember thinking you'd done a great job bringing her up . . . and that you two seemed to have a great bond.

When I saw the little video of her driving a few days ago, again
I was struck by how like you she was. Little facial gestures,
movements of the head that were you to a T. She would have
been about the age you were when we met, so it was like seeing
a young Rosie, and it made me smile.

But the most eloquent comments came from the many young
people who Mia befriended. From school friend Nicholas:

Mia will always be a huge part of growing up to me and I'll
take a lot of her personality and confidence with me along my
journey. Your daughter touched a lot of people and is loved
by many. She had a lot of strength that she obviously gained
from you and I hope you take that with you in the next couple
of weeks.

And this simple note from travelling companion Anna Boo:

Hi Rosie, I woke up to your post. It turns me into a speechless
crying child. I just wanted you to know I loved her so much,
we all did.

My advice to her friends was to raise a glass to her memory, dry
their tears and celebrate her life. Laugh, dance on the table, but
above all, build bridges in her name. Mia was notoriously blunt
and many of them would have experienced her sharp wit, but she'd
tried so hard not to let the sun go down on discord.

Mia couldn't dance anymore, or have babies, or travel, or fulfil
her ambitions. They had to dance for her now.

8

Bringing Mia Home

As we disembarked at Brisbane airport, I noticed a line of policemen in the tunnel leading to the arrivals area. We had been promised an escort to the hotel and there they were. We must have looked like we were being arrested for some heinous crime, but we were all past caring. The police had been well briefed and refused to answer my first question: 'How's Tom Jackson?'

Megan Hunt from the consulate was there to meet us, and she told us Tom hadn't survived. It was devastating to hear that this heroic man had died trying to save Mia's life. I dissolved again into the hopeless sobbing that had plagued me for most of the flight.

The police escort was far and above what we were expecting. It took us from Brisbane airport all the way to our hotel in Surfers Paradise. The journey was further than I'd realised, but I was to learn that this was par for the course in Australia – everything is always further than you realise. I felt quite embarrassed that we'd put the police to such trouble.

Jordyn and Jesse had booked us in to a hotel suite in the Hilton overlooking the main drag in Surfers. Jordyn lived in the same street, in the lovely apartment she had shared for a couple of months with Mia before she left for her farm work. Just like we did now, Mia and Jordyn had had views over the ocean. Our hotel suite was actually a self-contained flat with all the appliances for self-catering, so at least we would be comfortable during out stay. Downstairs there was a gym and pool with a sauna, and we made frequent use of these facilities in an attempt to relax during our first days in Australia. The rest of the family were staying in the same hotel, so every now and then we'd get a phone call from Nicola who used us as an escape route when she needed a gin and tonic away from her abstinent dad and gran.

Shortly after arriving we were visited in our suite by the six-foot-five burly regional crime coordinator Ray Rohweder from Queensland Police Service, who came to give us a thorough account of Mia's last hours.

Having investigated all of Mia's private possessions, he pointed out that there was nothing to link her to her killer, and no sense in which she had been in any way to blame. We knew this already, because if there had been a connection between them, Mia would either have told us or it would have emerged in the press, but to hear it from an authority figure was one of the comforting moments in this nightmare.

We also learnt that Ayad had been a respected employee, a team leader on the farm, and it was his second visit to the hostel to work. We learnt that he was generally well liked but had started to present with signs of mental health issues before Mia and Tom arrived, and he was now believed to be suffering from schizophrenia. He had been tested for drugs, and cannabis was found in his system.

As he was telling us this, Ray surprised us all when he broke down himself and wept. He told us that he had suffered a personal loss a few months previously – his sister had died – and he knew what we were going through only too well.

Surfers Paradise is basically a holiday resort for youngsters, and I could see the attraction for a young, pretty girl on the trip of a lifetime. The Hilton was in a street in central Surfers, so there were plenty of bars, restaurants and clubs, and it turned out that Mia's workplace had indeed been within spitting distance from her home. Although I'd worried about the cost of her beautiful apartment, it was actually just about affordable for her when shared with Jordyn. At least it meant she experienced some comfort and luxury in her last weeks on earth. The sea-view apartment had been kept on by Jordyn, and was still home to the forbidden tabby kitten Leo.

Stewart and I met up with Jordyn and Jesse on that first evening. Frankly, they looked absolutely terrified. I'd had some contact with them already, but part of it had been to beg them not to share pictures of Mia and themselves in their work outfits on their social media profiles, or at least to check their privacy settings. They were expecting me to be very hard work, and I had been expecting girls with few qualifications or ambitions who enjoyed the limelight and played on their looks.

Gradually we overcame our prejudices about each other, and I began to understand why Mia loved them so much and had wanted to spend a second year in their company. Both were bright and capable: Jordyn wanted a career in sports training, while Jesse was looking to study medicine. Both saw their work at the club as a means to an end, as they were taking home healthy wage packets and were able to save for their studies and travel. They were fun and delightful to spend time with, but they had their sights on their futures, much like Mia.

They had also taken the situation in hand in Australia, so that there was very little left for me to do. They had organised a chapel service and a get-together afterwards, and were putting the finishing touches to their speeches for the ceremony.

My main reason for making contact with Mia's friends was to help them to celebrate her life, rather than grieve her death, and to that end we arranged a trip to Byron Bay together, a place Mia had enjoyed very much on a visit with two other friends, Jameson and Misha.

After we parted, Jesse messaged me to apologise if she had stared at me too much, but I was 'SO like Mia' in my mannerisms and behaviour, she'd been shocked! I don't think either Mia or I realised this about ourselves, but I've heard it many times now, usually when I meet someone for the first time who knew Mia.

The biggest decision for me now was whether to view Mia's body. I had decided emphatically against it, as I felt I didn't need to. I am not afraid of death and had derived great comfort from being with my father as he died, and I had not wanted to leave his side in any hurry. But my father wasn't stabbed brutally several times, he was still warm, and aged eighty-four.

Mia's nan, Ruby, tried to make me reconsider as she thought I needed 'closure'. What is this closure? Acceptance of death? I didn't accept it. Mia was alive in my heart. She told me every day what to do. Did it matter that I talked about her in the present tense? Did closure mean I would forget her?

Others had told me that if I saw her it would eclipse all other images. But how could it wipe out the image of Mia tottering off on her first independent bike ride? Or acting out a demanding role on stage? Or Mia coming home from her first science lesson at her new school, blown away by a teaching style she could actually comprehend? Nothing will eclipse those memories.

And could I live to regret not seeing her? I just didn't know, and for once Mia, who generally had an opinion on everything, was silent. In the end, I decided to view her body, because it was the brave thing to do.

Mia looked like she was asleep. I stared and stared because I was sure that every time I looked away she moved. It reminded me of a visit to a waxworks museum, where you send a child to ask directions of a fake policeman. The pretty creature lying there in Mia's best dress was a perfect replica. But Mia wasn't there.

We left quickly. I hadn't found closure, and I hadn't found Mia. I was desolate.

Luckily I was with the New Zealand branch of the family, my lovely, sensible and highly supportive cousins Gill and Sara, so I couldn't head to a bar to order gin, although the temptation to greet oblivion for a few hours was strong.

Before us lay the longest beach I'd ever seen. Endless miles of sand lapped by a feisty, furious ocean which crashed in my ears and prevented me articulating my thoughts. After a coffee, I left the others sitting in the dunes and headed down to the surf.

And there she was!

At last I felt Mia's presence there on the sand, and in the wild, majestic waves. I waded into the water and she was there trying to surf with Jameson. I turned around and she was lying in a bikini being photographed by a friend. From afar she was running and laughing with the girls from the bar, then collapsing into heaps of giggles. She was everywhere! The crashing of the waves chimed with my grief and I started to cry and just couldn't stop. I ran and ran along the empty beach, sobbing and laughing like some crazy thing because she was there, and she always would be there. And I knew then I'd be back, and Mia would still be there.

After that I felt strong. I could do all the things I'd resolved to do for the ceremony the next day. I shopped until I found the perfect outfit, blowing a month's food budget on a designer black and floral dress. We found some jewellery Mia would approve of and then, a new experience for me, I headed to a nail bar. Mia would have been so proud: 'Ooh . . . get you, Momma!'

A minor aspect of the press coverage in some of the less salubrious papers had been the portrayal of the Bedroom nightclub as a strip joint, and I was determined to visit and find out for myself. The Bedroom Lounge Bar is situated on the main street in Surfers, which essentially is a row of restaurants, clothing and souvenir shops and other nightclubs. Jesse, Jordyn, Stewart and I ate together in one of Mia's favourite restaurants next door to the Hilton, then walked the 200 metres or so to the club. I was full of anticipation and some dread about the kind of place I was visiting. Had Mia been some kind of high-class callgirl for her last couple of months before heading to North Queensland?

I was quite shocked on entering, therefore, to find myself in what looked like a secondary school end-of-year disco, but without the glamour. The youngsters who frequented the bar were dressed for comfort rather than style and favoured dance moves usually the preserve of dads at weddings. The decor was reminiscent of a bedroom, true, complete with beds around the raised dais, but that's where the promise of sex ended. It was certainly less raunchy than a night on the town in the high street of any major British city.

As a consequence of the recent tightening of laws governing the hospitality industry, which controls opening hours and excessive drunkenness, there were two policemen in the bar, in uniform, perusing the dance floor. The manager, Brad, told me they were subjected to routine checks on many aspects of their business practices.

Jesse and Jordyn told me their parents shared my concerns about the establishment, and didn't like the outfits the waitresses had to work in. It seemed to me to be unnecessary to attract the clientele, which was essentially young adults out to party. But what did I know? It was a successful business, and Mia had respected Brad at least for his relaxed but firm management style. She'd told me she felt safer working there than she ever had in the UK, because she could be assured of immediate backup if she made a complaint about a customer.

The girls came back to our apartment at the Hilton and we talked candidly about their love for Mia. Jesse is of Maori descent and she and Mia had shared experiences of belonging to a minority cultural group in a majority white society. They kept marvelling at how alike Mia and I were, not just in looks and gestures but also in our attitudes and our humour. They described Mia delivering a killer punchline with perfect timing. I was so proud to be compared to my girl.

I loved these beautiful, strong, capable women and looked forward to welcoming them to Britain. I knew Mia's friends there would give them a true Derbyshire welcome.

Jesse explained that in her culture the dead are kept among the living for days, and they are touched, kissed and embraced as if they are alive. For this reason Jesse had insisted on visiting Mia's body and taking Jordyn and Jameson with her. Jordyn said that Jesse had led the way in holding Mia's hand and kissing her that day, and that she and Jameson followed suit. I found this incredibly moving.

9

Memorials

LOVELY AS BOTH MIA'S MEMORIAL CEREMONIES WERE, THEY ARE all a bit of a blur to me. I was on autopilot, meeting and greeting, but not present in any real sense of the word.

In Australia, Jesse and Jordyn had selected the perfect location: a tiny chapel in a deep-cut valley with a garden full of flowers, and a waterfall playing behind a clear glass window. Mia's Gold Coast friends read their testimonies while a slide show of photographs played, and then we released balloons into the sky. Representatives from the UK High Commission, including the British High Commissioner Menna Rawlings, and Megan Hunt from the consulate attended and laid wreaths, and later conveyed condolences from Australia's prime minister Malcolm Turnbull, who had apparently been following Mia's story closely in the press. We left Australia after what felt like the longest ten days of our lives, having been deeply impressed by the compassion and kindness we had encountered there.

Five days after our return to the UK, another service was held
to celebrate Mia's life. We were lent a white marquee on a lawn
down at a local hotel, Alison House, which was a lovely gesture on
the part of the business, but it did look very like a wedding venue.
Despite the commitment I had formulated over the days since
Mia's death to never entertain 'what ifs' and 'if onlys', I couldn't
help but wish we were indeed there in our best dresses, like so many
families had been that summer, for a wedding rather than a funeral.
We'd all dressed so brightly in Mia's memory, the only thing that
was missing were the bride and groom.

The UK celebration was also where we first met Les and Sandra
Jackson. Ten days later, accompanied by my cousin Mary, I travelled to Congleton for Tom's funeral.

If you had to be thrown into a situation as devastating as that in
which we found ourselves, your one hope would probably be that
the other people involved were as kind, funny and compassionate
as Les and Sandra. These two Liverpudlians had met as teenagers
and were strong both as a couple and as individuals, and they have
now become friends and allies of ours. Their family unit comprised
of Tom, the eldest, who was the image of Les but probably got his
height from Sandra's side. Next came Liv, who was supposed to be
embarking on her teacher training, but was so devastated by Tom's
death that she had to shelve it for the time being. Daniel was the
baby of the family, and like Liv he absolutely adored his brother
and took his loss as a deep blow. Les and Sandra are both Liverpool
United supporters and churchgoers and had evidently received
huge support from those two communities. Their spiritual lives
were guided by a wonderful pastor, Heather Kemball, who prayed

with them and stood by them and also reached out to me to offer condolences and support.

After having kept my composure through Mia's two ceremonies, it was only when I had no particular role to play that I broke down and cried my eyes out. It was good to see the Jacksons in their own community and to meet some of their lovely friends.

Les's eulogy to Tom was funny, touching and deeply moving, and I learnt a huge amount about them as a family, and about their eldest son. Tom was a strong character with great integrity who easily made friends and was admired by all for his outspokenness and bravery. No one had been surprised that he had died trying to save someone's life, because that was the kind of person he was; he would always be the first to put himself in the line of fire if he saw something he disagreed with or someone who needed protecting.

Sandra and Les would become campaigners with me in the months to come, and I'm proud to count them now among my friends. I look forward to a future when we're still in touch and able to meet up, when maybe the sadness we naturally evoke in each other will have been replaced by a sense of achievement and the thought that we have made a difference to the lives of other backpackers like Tom and Mia.

One discovery I made at the ceremony in Australia emerged out of the blur of those weeks, from a brief conversation with the brother of Chris Porter. It was Chris who had accompanied Mia to Home Hill Backpackers, and he'd ended up on crutches as a consequence of trying to save lives that night. His brother had settled in Australia some time earlier, and informed me that there were all sorts of scams surrounding the 88 days; apparently some young backpackers didn't manage to complete their days and gain their second year as a result of this. He cited people working on farms which weren't eligible to sign people off, and then not even being paid. I'd been horrified to learn that this government scheme wasn't better regulated.

This chimed with a conversation I'd had with Mia's friend Jameson about Mia and farm work. The pair had dated for a while, and afterwards remained friends. I knew Mia loved him, and was very happy that the break-up was mutual and amicable, and that she'd planned on her return from her farm work to share a flat with him on the Gold Coast while she found her feet again. I'd realised he was a kind and sensitive soul from what she'd told me about him, and he's proved that sensitivity to me since then.

I'd asked him about Mia's attitude to farm work and he said she really hadn't wanted to do it. He told me she'd been aware of the issues and exploitation and that she had refused to go strawberry picking in Caboolture for fear of sexual exploitation, because they only wanted girls. In retrospect, this could have been because girls were considered to have a lighter touch, but it suggested she was being careful. Jameson said that she had wanted to create a website to help people with their 88 days, and we talked about the possibility of creating such a site, making it a hub for reviews of farms and working hostels. I was determined to look into this more closely on my return to the UK.

10

Embarking on the Campaign Trail

MIA WILL ALWAYS BE APPROACHING HER TWENTY-FIRST BIRTHDAY, on a beach, playing games with her friends, dancing and laughing with babies and toddlers in the sunshine, healthy and strong, and looking her head-turning, devastatingly beautiful self. I don't pity Mia unless I dwell on the manner of her death and a lifetime unlived.

Whenever grief overwhelmed me, it was myself I pitied, and I spent hours doing just that. Between 3 and 5 am I often sat on the balcony in Australia, and again back in Derbyshire, out on the decking watching the day break over the misty valley, and wept and wept for my loss. It was definitely cathartic, but I needed to transform that grief into something. Apart from anything else, it was really cold out on that decking as winter approached.

I suppose people saw my mission as one of transforming grief into bravery, and righting wrongs. I was told it would be a lifetime's work, and that I was threatening the basis of the Australian economy, and all the authorities would want was for me to go away.

I had already encountered anger and disdain from people with a vested interest in the hostels in Australia. But I wasn't brave or stupid, remarkable or deluded. I just didn't give a damn anymore, and that made me untouchable.

It's not that I didn't care whether I lived or died. I have always had a positive mindset and am lucky enough never to have suffered badly from depression, and I was now drawing on that strength to keep me positive. I could still take pleasure in the beauty of nature: in sunlight playing on water as it tumbled over the rocks of the Derwent River, or in the balletic movements of our lurcher Nancy when she was released from the lead in a field, and the clown-like tumbling of our clumsy collie pup Fynn as he tried to out-manoeuvre her. It's just that I no longer feared failure, disgrace or public humiliation.

What I planned to do, I would do to honour Mia. It was in that sense that she was with me, and it meant I could do things I thought were beyond me. I wasn't sure I could control my emotions well enough to speak at her memorial service, but when it came to it I knew that Mia would help me contain my grief until the end. I didn't think I could face speaking to large audiences on radio or TV, but I would do what was needed. I felt that I could try to change the world, and whether or not I succeeded was immaterial, I had to try.

And so I started campaigning. I knew it wouldn't prevent the dismissive treatment of immigrants the world over, not even on my own doorstep. I have always had a global perspective, having lived in Turkey and visited India and Morocco, witnessing the rub of wealth and acute poverty for a few years in my twenties. Having had many close friends from the Middle East I was perhaps more aware of the conflict in Syria and how it has devastated an entire country, and I felt the plight of those who first lose someone – or even everyone – they held dear, and then are faced with a desperate fight for survival while dealing with their grief. By comparison I was indeed privileged. I could choose the path I took in this process of recuperation. By that same token I was able to harness the initial media interest to highlight some of the issues that exposed Mia and Tom to the crime committed on that dark night. I intended to campaign for better regulation of the 88 days, and gradually I worked out a set of demands with the support of the Jackson family.

Firstly we wanted registration of employees on the 88 days, so that it would be evident who was taking part at any time, and how many were involved in the scheme. We were also asking for a centralisation of work allocation by a government agency, matching job applicants with job vacancies and sending workers to farms based on vacancies. If young people were kept waiting for work, time spent should count towards the 88 days, or at least their stay should be at the expense of the hostel owner. In theory we thought this would prevent hostels being overcrowded for profit and young people from waiting inordinate amounts of time for work. All workers should be issued information in electronic format of their workplace rights, their rights regarding treatment in the event of an accident and their employer's health and safety responsibilities, and be given numbers for the Fair Work Ombudsman, the state's rape crisis centre, the Salvation Army and other support services. We wanted follow-up calls to be carried out by the government agency to ensure participants have received health and safety induction, fair – and all of – their wages, and that living conditions met government requirements. We also wanted to see a register of workplaces allowed to participate based on frequent, unannounced government inspections ensuring the provision of such basics as workplace insurance, on-site portaloos and water supplies, and the availability of medical kits and trained first aiders. Accommodation should be certified as meeting industry specifications of fire safety and be fit for purpose (clean and infestation-free).

By highlighting the current injustices – relatable to Westerners as their own youngsters take wing – I hoped it would be a step along the road for better treatment of all migrants when they found themselves in new and uncertain situations. The abuse of those made vulnerable by their displacement and loss is a disgusting indictment of our modern civilisation, and I am entirely admiring of those who work to end these injustices. I would become privileged to meet people whose life's work had been entirely this, and I'd be amazed at their resilience and mental fortitude.

But first I had to do my research on the 88 days scheme itself. On my return to the UK I joined a few backpacker groups in Australia and started to watch what was being said about the program. I also searched for press coverage, read articles and generally tried to get a feel for the situation. What I discovered was an astonishing state of affairs, and one of which most Australians, never mind Europeans, were completely unaware.

Initially I just found a few articles about isolated incidents, but nobody seemed to be joining up the dots. It was difficult for the youngsters to speak up because they were so vulnerable to further abuse, or they didn't trust the authorities. In the outback they might not even have the connectivity to reach the authorities, or their family and friends elsewhere. Eventually I came across reports made long before I came on the scene, in particular a thorough documentation of the exploitation of backpackers in the state of

Victoria commissioned by the Victorian government and written by an academic called Professor Anthony Forsyth, and a parliamentary inquiry into the practices of the labour hire industry in Queensland, published in June 2016. I realised I would be adding my voice to a growing clamour for change, which was a much more comfortable place to be than a lone wolf, crying in a wilderness.

Specifically I was campaigning for regulation of the 88 days, which would include a register of workplaces which had been inspected and were compliant with health and safety regulations, but I also wanted on-the-spot, unannounced inspections, and registration of backpackers on the scheme, partly to assess the numbers who embarked on it and failed in their endeavours to achieve the coveted 88 days, but also in order to collate statistics of accidents and mortalities. Some generic government-led training in what to expect in an Australian workplace, and how to deal with natural threats such as intense heat and the notorious Australian wildlife would also be welcomed.

The main reason I decided to campaign so early after Mia's death was that I knew I needed to strike quickly to capitalise on the media interest. After some local press work with Radio Derby and *East Midlands Today* on TV, the first interview of real note was with Jane Garvey of BBC Radio 4's *Woman's Hour*. It was 28 September 2016, and so close on the heels of Mia's and Tom's deaths that Jane was concerned about whether I'd be able to speak at all. The first thing she did was to offer me the option of backing out. Having travelled down to the studio in London from Derbyshire for the opportunity, there was no way that was going to happen.

Jane asked great questions, and I felt I did the campaign and Mia credit, especially when it was chosen from the week's stories and featured in their weekend digest. Jane told me afterwards that I'd spoken well, despite my self-deprecating comments about not being a public speaker. In the months to come I realised what an impact the interview had made with such a prestigious radio program, as many people contacted me as a consequence of it.

One significant event that took place in those early days was when I was contacted by a woman called Mary Gaskin. She said she worked for the Gangmasters Licensing Authority (now the Gangmasters and Labour Abuse Authority), a UK public body regulating the supply of workers to the agricultural industries in order to protect them from exploitation, and that what I was doing was related to the work she did. Mary also told me that more than a decade earlier she had found herself working out in Australia prior to the 88 day stipulation, in conditions she found highly exploitative. When she'd realised what the rate of pay per bucket meant in real terms, namely a few dollars a day, she stood up and said as much out loud, in the middle of a field. Her colleagues had immediately advised her to be quiet, as they said she would be left there by the farmer and made to walk several kilometres back to the hostel to pick up her belongings. She also talked about overcrowding and lack of compliant fire exits and extinguishers. Being Mary, she noticed these things even as a young adult, but her attention would have been focused as this was fairly close to the terrible Childers Palace Backpackers Hostel fire of 2000 in Queensland, in which fifteen young people died.

For a while I was really confused by Mary's message and didn't understand the significance. The term 'gangmaster' suggested modern slavery, and that seemed to me too extreme to describe the levels of exploitation in Australia. However, I agreed to a meeting, and Mary came over to Cromford one afternoon with her son Freddy.

Mary and I talked about the origins of the GLAA and her role of enforcement officer with arresting powers. I discovered the organisation works with the police to bring cases of modern slavery and abuse to light. In the UK there are laws and penalties in place, so perpetrators can be imprisoned and prevented from employing others in future. The GLAA had managed to harness the power of the media to discourage other employers from exploiting workers. Nothing of this kind existed as yet in Australia, and even deaths through negligence on farms attracted derisory fines for those responsible.

I showed Mary some of the data I had already collected and she said she saw aspects of modern slavery in some of the 88 day situations. One feature that particularly alerted her, she said, was the retention of passports. I hadn't reckoned on its significance, but Mary pointed out that with no passport it becomes very difficult to leave a hostel – a passport is your means of identity, and it's required by all subsequent accommodation and by employers to prove you're working legally in a foreign country. In fact, the confiscation of passports was actually illegal in Australia, but I found out later that it was not illegal to retain a passport if it was handed over freely by the client.

Mary also talked to me about debt bondage, which is where a worker is always working to pay off a supposed 'debt' to an employer, whether it be for accommodation, equipment, clothing, transport – anything work-related. I had learnt that this was another common practice in Australia: working hostels advertise non-existent employment in order to fill their beds. They take deposits and a couple of weeks' rent up front, possibly passports too.

Come Monday morning the workers find out they're in a queue, and they need to wait for work. This wait can be a matter of days or even weeks. When they do get work, it might be a couple of days a week, as the work is being eked out to keep them indebted and to keep the hostel full. Basically, teams of workers end up working for zero gain, the only winners being the farmers and hostel owners.

Thanks to Mary Gaskin, Paul Broadbent readily agreed to meet me. Paul was the chief executive officer of the Gangmasters and Labour Abuse Authority and he imbued me with a real sense of direction and purpose.

I met him in October 2016 at their office in Nottingham. Paul was charismatic and obviously incredibly well-versed in the area of worker exploitation. He was deeply sympathetic and amazed at the fact I could contemplate helping others, given what I'd so recently been through. He listened to what I had to say, and he acknowledged as Mary had done previously that the 88 days regime created a vulnerability in backpackers that meant they were highly susceptible to exploitation. Paul understood my frustrations completely, having fought so hard to change the attitude to workplace abuse and modern slavery in the UK. He agreed to support the campaign and I was delighted: he would become an indomitable ally – it didn't get much better in terms of support. I knew that with Paul's assistance I could one day achieve my objective of regulation of the 88 days.

That month, Australia's Fair Work Ombudsman produced a report of some weight that highlighted most of what I had discovered for myself about the 88 day scheme, although it concentrated more on wage theft than the safety aspects which motivated me. It stated:

The FWO regards 417 visa workers as especially vulnerable due to the difficulties in understanding and exercising their entitlements because of age and language barriers. In particular, their vulnerability is increased if they choose to undertake an 88-day placement, because of the remoteness of their working location and their dependence on employers to obtain eligibility for a second year visa . . . The FWO received information from visa holders, stakeholders and the public identifying a range of concerns suggesting exploitation of 417 visa holders, including instances of:

- underpayment and or non-payment of wages
- visa holders offering, or being induced to offer, payment to employers and third parties for assistance to gain a second-year work rights visa
- an increased dependency on the employer by the visa-holder seeking employment during the 88 day specified work requirement of the 417 visa program in order to secure a second-year visa and stay in Australia
- sexual harassment and workplace health and safety issues
- employers recruiting workers with the offer of unpaid work to meet the second-year visa eligibility requirements
- visa holders working for free in exchange for non-certified accommodation programs.

At that time, I received a call from a woman saying she was Michal's mum, asking if she could come visit me. Mia and Michal had been boyfriend and girlfriend when they were both sixteen, and remained friends to her death. He had often stayed over at our house, but I had never met Atessa before as she lived a distance away in a cottage in the hills of Derbyshire.

As soon as I opened the door, she burst into tears. I was somewhat bemused. Two months after Mia's death, there was still a general rawness among Mia's friends but inevitably there had been a tailing off of others' outpourings of grief. We talked for some time, and I learnt more in the months to come about Atessa's own loss, and her close relationship with Mia, whom she adored.

She asked about the campaign, and I explained what I'd found out about the 88 day scheme and the press interest I'd garnered so far. She suggested we start a petition to demand better regulation. She even helped me to word it, which made me laugh as she still had a slight Polish accent, but the structure she suggested was better than my original. The petition went live that day, and included an open letter to Malcolm Turnbull for good measure which outlined the accumulation of negative issues around the implementation of the 417 Working Holiday Visa Program. It read:

6 October 2016

I am the mother of Mia Ayliffe-Chung, the young woman who was fatally stabbed at a workers' hostel in Queensland in August this year, along with her co-worker Tom Jackson. Both Mia and Tom were 417 Working Holiday Visa holders and were undertaking days of specified paid work in the region to become eligible for a second-year visa. Like many other young people, they were seeking new and enriching experiences abroad whilst working under the provisions of this program.

I travelled to Australia after Mia's death, and became aware of an accumulation of negative issues around the implementation of the 417 visa system, which I believe may have

contributed indirectly to the deaths of Mia and Tom. You will
be aware that these issues have been described in the media
and – most recently – in the report of the Fair Work
Ombudsman's two-year inquiry into the wages and conditions of people working under the 417 Working Holiday Visa
Program.

The Inquiry report describes widespread illegal and
unscrupulous treatment of 417 visa holders. Practices include
underpayment and non-payment of wages, and unlawful
deductions from wages. The report also identifies issues of sexual harassment and other exploitative employer behaviours
in isolated and remote workplaces. It cites cases of employers and hostels withholding passports without authority.
Health and safety issues in workplaces are also frequently
ignored (for example my daughter had no safety instruction
or briefings on wildlife when working in the Queensland cane
fields, notorious for dangerous snakes). The inquiry found
that even the recent 2015 reforms around paid work are 'open
to circumvention by unscrupulous employers through false
record-keeping and unauthorised deductions'.

Most 417 visa workers are young people. The report highlighted the vulnerable nature of this group exposed to rogue
employers and the current operation of the 417-visa program
is creating a culture of exploitation in many remote locations.
Here accommodation provided can be poor, and vulnerable
visa holders in competition for work are under pressure to
agree to work illegally and in potentially unsafe situations.

There is often limited phone and internet coverage and
the inquiry concluded that such isolation also 'creates an
additional level of vulnerability'.

Employers of 417 visa holders are not monitored and there are no penalties for them under migration law for contravening workplace laws.

I believe that these are the type of working conditions which generate an aggressive and overheated atmosphere amongst young workers, and that this contributed to the febrile environment in which the fatal stabbings of Mia and Tom took place.

I know that working holiday-makers are an important part of Australia's tourism industry and a key source of labour in regional agriculture. I also fully understand that these situations are not all typical of what happens in Australian farms.

However, as long as some unscrupulous employers can break the law with impunity, substantial dangers exist for visa holders. This also brings considerable reputational damage to both law-abiding employers and to the whole 417 program abroad.

Your government has a stated policy of protecting vulnerable workers and I welcome the establishment of the Migrant Workers' Taskforce, whose remit is to swiftly rectify instances of worker exploitation.

To prevent possible further tragedies and in the interests of all 417 visa workers I would urge your government to take account of the findings of the inquiry report by ensuring that all employers' practices are closely monitored to ensure compliance with the law and that enforcement action is taken where needed.

Yours sincerely,
Rosie Ayliffe

I posted the petition on Facebook along with a post explaining who I was, about Mia's death and why I was campaigning. I was keen to garner signatures, but along with the first trickle came a host of stories from backpackers. Responses came through social media from people already working in this field, including two Australians called Rob Daniels and Robyn Horvath. Both had welcomed struggling backpackers into their homes and had stories to tell about exploitation and abuse. Rob was the owner of a well-run, compliant hostel in Western Australia, which often turns into a refuge for backpackers fleeing difficult situations. Robyn was a teacher in the state of Victoria who had offered backpackers refuge in her home, and had already petitioned the National Union of Workers to highlight the treatment of backpackers in her state.

Some of the early messages I received from backpackers were indicative of the issues. One described working for a woman in a place infamous among backpackers for being 'full of corruption and scams'. Her practices included deductions from agreed rates of pay (so taking $3 off each crate of spring onions picked, resulting in a take-home amount of $9 instead of $12 per crate). Accommodation was raided by the police, officials from the immigration department and Fair Work when reports of her selling drugs to backpackers surfaced. When informed that a 417 visa holder intended to leave, she responded by saying she wasn't going to sign off on the days worked, resulting in a loss of twelve days not recorded for that worker.

Another testimony in response to that first post of mine was from someone who had been in a coastal region of Queensland, and was initially promised a pumpkin/squash job but after signing papers and contracts was told they had to do tomatoes for a day or two, which turned into a month and paid 17 cents a kilo. The climate was unforgiving: a minimum of 30 degrees that summer, with a working day of between nine and twelve hours, so on the first day earnings were $64. It was impossible to cover the rent during the first two weeks, which in turn trapped them there for a month until they could earn enough for the ticket out. These eye-witness accounts used the term modern day slave labour, and recounted how many are unlucky and get caught in a scam or in having to re-do their days, or simply give up and go home due to the treatment received.

I was moved to read comments such as:

I have seen the news regarding your family and I am sorry for your loss and thank you for actually acting and trying to help us.

I was introduced to the concept of woofing, in which backpackers work for food and accommodation instead of money. Two guys and a girl who'd been staying on a woofing property moved on to a job advertised on a backpackers job board, as they were promised the chance to earn $21.60 an hour and have the farm sign off the second working holiday visa for them. On arrival they had to hand in their car keys and passports and pay two weeks' accommodation up front plus a bond for the room ($1050 in total for three people). On Monday work commenced. They were picked up at 5 am and worked all day, to be back at home again at 5 pm. That is when they found out their earnings for that day – $50 per person for working ten hours with two hours of travelling! When they went to confront the hostel owner and demanded their money and passports, she refused, so they went to the police, but there wasn't much they were going to do for them either. It was only after getting angry with the hostel owner that they were able to leave with their passports and a refund.

A few days later I received this message, which seemed to illustrate many of the prevalent issues, but also brought home to me how aware backpackers themselves are of the pitfalls of the 88 days scheme:

I travelled to the hostel after being reassured on the phone there was plenty of work for me, there was a bed reserved for me and rent was $160 a week. Upon arrival I was told of the $300 bond needed in cash and had the rules explained to me, including a fee of $10 a day to drive you to the farm. I was then told it could take a while for there to be work available to me; worst case would be a two-week wait. I was given my sheets, a few pieces of cutlery and shown my bed. Twelve bunk beds crammed into a room adjoined to multiple other rooms via what used to be closets and cluttered storage areas. On speaking to other backpackers I was told I would more than likely be here for more than the three months. Some had been there for almost half a year as the work is spread out to a couple of days a week to keep you there for much longer, paying full rent.

I had to sleep on a mattress 2 inches thick which provided no protection from the old wood of the broken bunk bed, and each morning I would wake up itchy and covered in peculiar bites. There was no clear escape route from any of the bedrooms in case of a fire, just one door at each end of the house, which was set out like a maze. I had one shelf for my belongings, which would often go missing; one bag in the fridge, which would have something taken from it every day;

and a box on the kitchen shelf which over time became an ant colony. There were three showers and three toilets to serve more than twenty-five of us in the house. Just two microwaves, two cooker tops, no pots and pans or bare-essential cooking equipment, or cleaning provisions. I was actually lucky to be sleeping in the house: two girls arrived having been promised a bed to be told they were to sleep in their car and pay $100 a week for the privilege. The house was old and dirty. Cockroaches in the bed and on the walls was a normality. 'Lights off' was at 10 pm. If we were outside the house after that time the owner would become irate and once sprayed us with a hose.

The drivers to the farms were other backpackers who paid a little less rent for doing drop-offs. One day one of the minibuses was pulled over by the police who asked the drivers about their insurance and licences. It was considered an illegal taxi service and they were not driving within the correct legal requirements.

The farm work was either picking or packing. The chilli farm was what most newcomers started on. We were given our buckets, told the best type of chilli to pick and dropped off in the middle of the field. There were no toilet facilities so we had to go in the field where we were picking. Even during our periods, women would have to go there and then. The packing jobs were a little more of a luxury, inside the warehouse out of the heat, and equipped with toilets. No proper personal protective equipment was provided and I knew of some girls losing the skin on the tips of their fingers.

Tensions were often high within the hostel about work theft, and relationships. Everyone coveted these farm jobs and was incredibly jealous of the lucky chosen few. People were often stressed about the days they still had to complete compared to the amount of time left on their visa. Bonds and relationships were made but could break down from living in such close quarters. People knew the owners had their 'favourite' backpackers who paid less rent for doing odd jobs and who always got placed on good farms. The atmosphere would more often than not be very bitchy and could easily turn nasty.

It seemed that whenever I went online, I'd read another public post highlighting the perils backpackers faced when trying to extend their visa. Some were upfront in their encouragement of others to just enjoy a one-year visa, as it was so often an ordeal to rack up 88 days. I read accounts of picking fruit where youngsters 'worked like slaves for nothing', of a backpacker taken away 'to clean a house where she was offered money for sex', and of factories closing down without warning, leaving backpackers out of pocket and scrambling to find work as their deadlines approached.

The Jackson family were even more aware than I was about the exploitation by this stage, as Tom had suffered from some of the issues which I was beginning to realise were prevalent across the industry. Tom informed his parents that he had been assured that work was plentiful and he could expect to be fully employed when he arrived.

After the petition went live, I asked Les and Sandra if Tom's name could be added to the campaign title, and they readily agreed. Thus began Tom and Mia's Legacy.

*

In November, I was invited back to the Gangmasters and Labour Abuse Authority headquarters in nearby Nottingham to meet Professor Anthony Forsyth, who was visiting from Australia. He described to a hall packed with GLAA enforcement officers the situation in Australia regarding the exploitation of migrant workers, which included students, undocumented workers and travellers on the 88 days scheme. He also pointed out the need for anti-slavery legislation in Australia, which to my astonishment did not yet exist. We met afterwards and he was warm in his assurances that I was on the right path in trying to shine a light on malpractices in Australia. Such encouragement, this time from an academic source, propelled me further along the path to keep campaigning for change.

In that first flush of campaigning enthusiasm I really believed I could change the world. However, I needed the right vehicle to get my message across. I was aware that the campaign led to awkward questions, such as, 'How can an English-speaking nation, a Commonwealth country no less, treat our young people in this way?' and, 'Wouldn't they just replace our youngsters with even more compliant workers, imported illegally, and abuse workers from developing nations instead?' Being allied to the GLAA would hopefully ensure that the campaign was about legislation and rights, rather than replacing one group of workers with another, who could potentially be treated even worse than the backpackers I was trying to help.

I was unlikely to get the traction required to make an impact in Australia if I pursued this on my own. Paul Broadbent of the GLAA advised me to work with the *Mail on Sunday* to help step things up a notch. Reluctant to invite the press into my home,

I arranged the hire of a suitable room at Alison House in Cromford, the lovely hotel where we'd held Mia's funeral tea. Nick Craven was a quality journalist with a history of solid investigative press work to his name, and we developed an easy rapport (though I haggled over the contract and insisted on seeing the article before it went to print). We were exactly the same age, give or take a month, had attended the same university at the same time and even lived in the same halls. I think this shocked us both: he was wondering how I'd fallen from such dizzy heights to become 'council house dwelling single parent (52) of murdered mixed-race child', while I was wondering how he'd fallen from such dizzy heights to become a tabloid reporter. I think we both learnt a lesson about prejudice over the next two days.

The whole interview must have taken more than three hours, with barely a break. The difficult bit for me was to make the connection between Mia's death and the campaign, because people still thought, as I did initially, that it was a random act of terror that came out of nowhere, so why was I campaigning about regulation? Nick grasped my position quickly. He had been drafted in superfast and wasn't really up to speed on the story, but he was bright, responsive and sensitive.

However, once I'd relaxed and felt Nick and I were bonding, Ian the photographer arrived. I might not be able to read a map, but I can read a face, and as he sat back, arms folded, and glared into space, I suspected he was sceptical, to say the least. I'm sure he'd met all types of characters on the planet, and I worried he thought I was a media whore, an attention-grabbing phoney who was using Mia's death to my own ends. I tried to ignore him for a while and carry on as if he wasn't there. I wished I had the nerve to ask him to leave, but I wasn't in a very assertive place.

You can't fake 'fighting back tears', it's either there or it isn't. I can be hard, too hard, sometimes, and I had already developed a steely determination not to cry in front of the press, which I've more or less succeeded at. But this was different. Nick's questioning was forensic, and being constitutionally incapable of lying, I told two completely strange men from another world all about my relationship with Mia, and many other events related to those years. Every now and then Nick would get a call from his editor at the *Mail on Sunday* and he'd ratchet the interview up with more emotional questions. Eventually I felt like I'd been cleaned with a pan scrub then finished off with a garden mower, and I struggled – but failed – to stop the tears.

I had to disappear out into the beautiful gardens for a cigarette. (A filthy habit. I was smoking – briefly – for the first time in five years.) Ian joined me.

I was embarrassed, and I told him what I thought about my tears: 'It's self-pity. It's just self-pity.'

He looked me squarely in the eye and said, 'No, it isn't. It's bereavement, it's a sense of loss.' I think we bonded at that moment.

We discussed some of the people Ian had photographed over the years, and I was surprised to discover that the list included every serving UK prime minister in his lifetime to date. I asked what he'd thought of them, and he replied that, surprisingly, and politics aside, John Major had probably been the most polite and charming of the lot of them.

The next day dawned early for me, as I'd reverted to the sleep patterns that had become so familiar during my trip to Australia and was up at 3 am. Just what you need in preparation for a photo-shoot. We'd arranged to meet at one of my favourite places in the area, a viewpoint on the High Peak Trail, but the start was something of a fiasco, as Nick, Ian, Koray (an additional agency photographer who was using the opportunity to take further photographs for their archives) and I attempted to arrive in the same place at the same time, with no phone signal between us and a sketchy knowledge of the geography of the area on their part. Factor in an inability to take simple instructions from a woman, and there you have it: chaos!

I was feeling more confident by the time we managed to meet up, as I'd been to the hairdresser in Wirksworth, who'd taken away the signs of grief and anxiety with a splendid makeover that made me look vaguely human.

Ian was delighted with the location I'd chosen, especially when a particular tree caught his eye. I had no idea what he was talking about until I realised that about 200 of the shots involved me leaning on said tree in various awkward postures. Nancy my lurcher was with us and viewed the whole affair sardonically with that typical lurcher attitude, occasionally deigning to join me, out-performing me every time with her elegant posture and grace. The absurdity of the situation was often too much and I kept grinning and snickering when I was supposed to be doing 'driven campaigner', but Ian and Koray were very patient. Koray is from Izmir, and I made him give all his instructions to me in Turkish, so that made it a little more bearable as I tried to get my ear back for the language (I wasn't allowed to talk).

A couple came past with more than average levels of curiosity. They weren't to be dismissed with my, 'I'm just a nobody, nothing to see here, honestly.' They kept questioning me until in the end I told them I'd lost Mia over summer. The woman paused for thought and then said, 'Well at least you've got a lovely dog!'

When they'd gone I turned to the guys and said, 'That has to be the most tactless thing anyone has said to me since Mia died!' And that was it, we couldn't stop laughing. It felt so good to have a deep belly laugh after the darkness of the preceding couple of days. Luckily the woman was well out of earshot by that stage.

True to his word, Nick sent me all his drafts of the article, as well as the final copy. His first draft was by far the best, it was compassionate and thoughtful. He concentrated on the campaign, kept the emotional content low-key, and showed a high level of comprehension of the link between Mia's death and my own grief and drive to make changes to the program.

In the end, the article was fine, despite the picture of Mia with a very dodgy haircut apparently executed with garden shears. On the whole, it was an interesting experience, and I can certainly recommend the *Mail*'s counselling service for bereaved mothers! In terms of the campaign, it raised our profile considerably – the *Mail* is one of the most widely read papers in the UK, but the Mail Online, where my interview also featured, is the most widely read publication in the world.

Two separate families – both friends of mine – contacted me to say their daughters had been involved in the 88 days program and would be willing to talk to the press about their experiences. The two young women were Joy Lakin, the daughter of a teaching colleague, and Jodie Keiana, the daughter of a novelist friend. By this stage I was in contact with a young English journalist who worked for the well-regarded news website and agency in Australia, news. com. She produced an article which was influential and sparked much press interest in Australia on the issues around the 88 days scheme, and then a further article for Mail Online incorporating Jodie's and Joy's stories and others from her own research.

These articles led to me acquiring a profile as a campaigner on social media, and I became the first port of call for many backpackers who wanted to air their grievances and to publicly identify dangerous operators. One of these was a young woman called Claire who happened to live close to fellow campaigner Robyn Horvath in Victoria, and who had recently given birth. She was struggling with an event in her past which had happened as a result of the 88 days.

On realising that she was pregnant with what turned out to be twins, Claire and her Australian boyfriend decided they would buy time through the 88 days, as they couldn't afford the $6000 required in Australia for a partner visa. She went to work on a remote farm, and, while sitting with the farmer in his ute, he propositioned her and tried to force himself on her.

She hit him hard with the nearest object, and escaped from the vehicle, running into a field with just her phone, from where she called her boyfriend. He turned up soon after and took her home, but she hadn't felt able to talk to him about the incident, because she worried he would retaliate and attack the farmer.

Claire had contacted me to say I was on the right track, as the scheme made backpackers vulnerable to sexual abuse, but it transpired that her current situation was worsened by the fact she had not completed her 88 days. She was in danger of being deported because her visa was about to run out, and she wouldn't even be able to get on a flight with both babies. I talked to Mary Gaskin from the GLAA in the UK and contacts in the Salvation Army in Australia (who I was learning did a lot of campaigning in this area), and meanwhile Robyn ran a check on Claire's credentials.

It transpired that they had friends in common who verified her story, so we started a fundraising campaign to pay for Claire's partner visa. She was incredibly grateful, although she couldn't talk about the events openly. (A couple of years down the line Claire gave birth again, and she called the new baby Mia Rose! What fantastic news of a birth into a happy family which would have otherwise potentially been riven by deportation.)

But alongside this positive story was news of the death of another backpacker, which affected me deeply. Marianka Heumann fell to her death in October 2016 after plunging thirteen floors down a ventilation shaft at a construction site in Perth. As soon as I read the report about her death on an industry website, I burst into tears. I felt in some way personally responsible, reasoning I hadn't campaigned hard enough to stop the death. I knew that it was preventable and that Marianka had been failed. Since our arrival in Derbyshire, Mia and I had enjoyed climbing outdoors together with local climbing clubs and one rule that we had learnt very early that was sacrosanct was you never removed your harness anywhere near a precipice – it was simply not something you did. We were informed that any induction into working at height would prioritise this message. On a later visit to Western Australia I expressed my belief on this matter to a union meeting. Later I saw a petition about the matter online, stating that Marianka, a diligent worker, had been employed for three months and yet had not learnt basic safety practices for working at height. She evidently believed that it was fine to forego safety procedures on that site, and she fell to her death.

Other deaths and horrible injuries reached me either anecdotally or through the press after inquests were completed: a young Taiwanese plumber who lost three fingers in farm machinery; an

Irish woman who was scalped and lost an ear when forced to clean a moving conveyor belt. It was startling to see just how dangerous farm work could be in Australia, and I had to wonder whether it was right that someone out there on a working holiday should risk their life for the privilege of being permitted to stay for a second year.

11

Downtime

In November 2016 Stewart and I took time out and flew to Portugal to visit friends Tom and Paula, a couple who'd lived in our home town and knew Mia from the time she minded children at the farm, as they were aunt and uncle to some of them. Paula was Portuguese, so they had settled there quite recently and bought a lovely property with a few acres of land on the enchanting Fóia mountain. We went to stay for a week before they came back to the UK for a visit, with the plan that I'd stay on and mind their cats on my own and have some downtime. I really needed to be alone with my thoughts and grieve in absolute peace. I still hadn't returned to my teaching job, and wasn't sure if I would ever be able to do so. Luckily my head teacher and the board of governors at the school were incredibly supportive of both my need to take time off and the campaign.

Just before I left Wirksworth, I received a message on social media that threw me. I learnt from Daniel Richards, an eye witness on that terrible night at Home Hill Backpackers, that Mia hadn't been unconscious from the first blow, as I had been led to believe by the police. She had run for shelter to the nearest bathroom, and had died slowly and, I now presumed, agonisingly, in the company of Daniel. A vision of this scene would recur at any moment, debilitating me absolutely. It still does. I was subsequently informed that the intense stress of the moment probably meant Mia felt no pain while she was dying, and I now believe from what I've read that this is probably true.

I wanted to meet the brave, tough-spirited Welshman with a deep sense of decency who had endured such terror on Mia's behalf, and to whom I am eternally indebted. I could only imagine what he was still going through months after the event, and I doubted he would come to terms with his experience any time soon. I wondered what provision was being made for him by the Australian government in terms of counselling, though I suspected the answer would be disappointing, given he was expected to complete his 88 days farm work and, incredibly, was still at Home Hill.

I had also heard that Ayad's trial wasn't going to take place, now or in the near future. He was being detained for as long as it took to determine whether he was genuinely suffering from mental health issues, or if he was dissembling.

I'd never needed to 'get away from it all' as much as I did then. This wasn't so much a holiday as an attempted retreat from everything except Mia's death. Six days into my stay I had stopped grinding my teeth, and started to actually listen properly to what was going on around me, instead of disappearing into deep reveries at every opportunity.

I'd had a week's induction into the mountain homestead and its surroundings. I knew which key was which, I knew how to get to the nearest shops. I was now comfortable taking Tom and Paula's four-wheel drive along the circuitous mountain routes, and I had identified presents to thank them for this opportunity to stay in one of the most beautiful parts of the world I had ever visited.

Then I received the news that my mother had passed away. Mum's death was not unexpected, due to the Alzheimer's she had been suffering from for the last few years, so there was a sense of relief mixed with loss. To be honest, at that time Mia's death eclipsed everything, and I found myself unable to comprehend how to deal with this added raft of emotions.

As usual, I woke in the early hours, in the dark at around 4 am. According to Ayurvedic tradition, 4 am is when you feel anxiety, so is a good time for meditation, while 6 to 8 am is when you experience grief and sadness. These hours are also a time of solitude, with only the distant barking of unknown hounds to disturb the peace of my mountainside retreat.

Early rising in the dark is kind of okay in your own house, because you know where to find light switches, the kettle, coffee cups and cigarette filters. At Fóia the first 40 minutes was spent fumbling around unfamiliar territory for any or all of these. But the darkness was warm, and the sweet smell of eucalyptus from the slopes outside was at last working its magic on my troubled soul.

The mountain is covered in every conceivable variety of fruit and brightly coloured flowers, and a recent rain storm had caused green shoots to appear everywhere. The place oozed with fecundity and the promise of sweet-tasting delights, from quince, olives and avocado to persimmon, figs, pomegranates, oranges . . . an endless list.

And the wildlife congregated accordingly. Owls were out hunting, and hooted their delight. Geckos, looking like miniature crocodiles, gathered around the external light and cleaned up on flies. And wild boar roamed the hills at night, occasionally crashing noisily through the undergrowth. So I was far from alone on the mountain. I had the world at my feet, and Mia in my heart.

Since Mia's death, and following the quieter, gentler passing of my mum, I had become something of an expert on grief or, more accurately, how to avoid grief's full effects by shelving it until a future date. My grieving for Mum had most definitely been shelved – not a recommended course of action for anyone, but perhaps it was my only real option if I wanted to carry on in any meaningful sense of the phrase.

I tried not to dwell on death too much in my daily life because of something I'd read in a book on Buddhism, which said that if you grieve your loss too deeply you can prevent your loved one from moving on and experiencing reincarnation. Of course, I have no idea whether or not this is true, but since watching *Extraordinary People: The Boy Who Lived Before* on YouTube years ago with Mia, I've not really been able to ignore the possibility. So much about Buddhism makes sense to me. Above all else, I had always suspected Mia had lived before.

Several times since her death, I'd been asked what I thought about the afterlife, although I didn't feel I was in a privileged position to know about it. I suppose it was something I was now contemplating more than most, as I didn't have a structured set of beliefs. The easy answer was that I didn't believe in an afterlife, but that's not strictly true.

I don't believe in heaven and hell. I think they're metaphors, born out of man's fear of the unknown. I don't picture Mia with Mum and Dad, sitting on some cloud with God and a bunch of angels. Mia's life certainly didn't lend itself to automatic entry into the Kingdom of Heaven, and I'm not prepared to accept the alternative.

At both of Mia's memorials we quoted the sonnet by Mary Elizabeth Frye, that Mia wasn't there, but was in the wind and rain, in the birds and in the stars. But if I'm honest, although I find this very beautiful and comforting, I don't believe it in a literal sense either. I was finding myself closer to Mia when in nature, and could visualise her more easily in beautiful places, especially on beaches, and in the hills, and now on Fóia mountain, which she would have loved for its fantastical film-set beauty, brightly coloured vegetation and abundant fruits. But did I really think her energy had been absorbed into all things natural?

Most of all, Mia was, and still is, a voice in my ear, in a way that no one else could or ever will be. We don't speak to each other; we don't need to. For most of Mia's twenty years, it was just Mia and me. I always felt that we were almost umbilically linked. I could walk into a room and, without looking up, Mia would sense something and say, 'What's wrong?' We went through grazing poverty together, we made sudden unplanned trips into the unknown together, we ate, laughed, loved and often fought together. I knew her opinions on everyone and everything, and not least on me. This is how I know precisely how she will be feeling about my every move. She 'tells' me in no uncertain terms when she thinks I'm being mean, fake or selfish, and when she's proud of me for rising above such pettiness. This is why I say she is my moral compass.

And so she lives on, a still, small voice of kindness and compassion, in a world which would otherwise be spinning out of control.

And I miss her. Not her physical presence, for I grew used to her absence during her trip to Australia, and was accustomed to communicating with her through social media. Since her death she has remained very much alive to me. I've talked to her friends for hours and they've evoked her presence in anecdotes, pictures, filmed clips of her travels around the world, a meticulously prepared twenty-first birthday party . . . and she was always there in the warmth and sunshine of summer.

This was intensified for me on Fóia mountain, when I sat outside in the warmth on Paula and Tom's terrace with a view towards the sea, tuning in and out of the beautiful song of cicadas and the tinkling of Paula's chiming bells, feeling Mia in the sunsets and sunrises and the healing warmth of the sun.

Winter had descended by the time I returned to the UK. It was gloomy, cold and dark and I struggled to find Mia anywhere. Now the reality was hitting home, and I was plagued with negative thoughts and images which I struggled to suppress.

Mum's funeral was an all-time low. I took a wrong turn on the way there, making Stewart (who was following behind in his own vehicle as he had to return to work the next day) and me late, so the whole procedure was halted as they waited for our arrival. The ceremony itself had been organised by my siblings, and Mark gave a beautiful eulogy. I broke down in tears and tried to find my way to the relative privacy of the sacristy, where we had changed into our robes back in the days I had been a member of the church choir, only to find the church's layout altered beyond recognition. This at least made me calm down, as I inspected the new fixtures with a critical eye. Rejoining the congregation, who were having tea and cakes in the north transept, I was greeted by a bearded man who I vaguely recognised. I struggled for a while and then realised it was my geography teacher from secondary school. During the ensuing conversation, I asked him whether he knew I'd become a teacher, and he replied drily, 'Yes, I had heard . . . the thought that sprang to mind was, "Poacher turned gamekeeper!"' I realised then that I had probably been more of a handful at school than I remembered!

Three times on the journey home from Mum's funeral I found myself shouting 'Stop it!' at the windscreen, to clear away the violent images in my head. Back home, the words of an Australian journalist who saw me through some wakeful hours in Portugal made me laugh through my tears when I cried. With the pragmatism and understanding of a woman who has grieved deeply herself, she messaged: 'Don't forget to moisturise, tears play havoc with your complexion!'

Symbolic things started to take on greater importance: the stained-glass window made in Mia's memory by a sweet stranger who was moved by our story; a gift from a neighbour of a ring containing Mia's ashes; the gift of photos of Mia's childhood in London, taken by a beloved friend, now also passed away; the kite tattoo designed by Jesse Tawhi's auntie, with the words, 'Fly high, Mia!' formed by its tail. Stewart and I, along with a friend of mine who had known Mia well, had booked a date to be tattooed with this design, and quite a few of our friends were following suit. This was something I never thought I'd do, but Mia would have absolutely loved the idea of me getting a tattoo!

Luckily I didn't have to face the decision most parents in my position agonise over: when, or even whether, to dismantle a dead child's bedroom. Mia had packed her belongings in boxes before she left (the house was being renovated and her room was next on the list for a makeover). Initially she wanted her badly packed boxes to be shipped to Australia, before she realised what it would actually cost, and that it would be cheaper to replace most of them. The only item that made the journey in the post was her MacBook, an eighteenth birthday present and source of literally thousands of photos of her and her friends. Before we decorated her room (to her careful specifications, of course) we put most of the boxes in the loft, so now we only had her clothing to deal with, and most of the nicer items were going to close friends who were small enough to fit into them. This was another source of comfort as I knew they would remember Mia when they wore them, and appreciate her carefully selected and – compared to my cautious budget – somewhat extravagant wardrobe.

The hardest part of that first year was Christmas Eve and the tree dressing. Anyone with children knows how every bauble brings back memories of Christmases past, and Mia and I had bought and made new ones each year. The tree dressing was such an important ritual to her that once, when I had had the effrontery to start without her, she stripped everything off and started from scratch! This year, the first Christmas without her, I tried to buy a new tree decoration at the local market and was overcome by a wave of grief and tears. How could a little ritual I used to love so much have become such a torment? Knowing Mia had planned to come home for Christmas and 'surprise' me and Stewart was delightful to hear back in summer, but now I had to suppress images of her appearing at the door with her arms thrown wide in anticipation of a hug, and some funny line to defuse our emotions.

By now I tried to start my day with three yoga salutes to the sun, and a few minutes of meditation in front of the Buddha seemed to calm my heart and soul for the day ahead. I would commune with Mia a fair bit too, just by focusing on her when I was making decisions, to hear the voice of reason that used to plague my every move when she was alive.

Something else that helped was to concentrate firmly on what I could change, rather than fretting over things I couldn't. By Christmas I think I had accepted that Mia was actually dead, that she wouldn't be coming through that door any time ever. But I could still celebrate her life with like-minded souls who under-stood her essence, who accepted who she was, imperfections and all, and loved her still, and forever, for everything that made her Mia. Her style and glamour, which would be thrown aside at the first snowfall in favour of woollens and wellies as she headed for the hills with anything she could find to use as a sledge. Her abil-ity to control a situation through sheer force of personality, like the time she got rid of some poor lad from her sixteenth birthday party because he threw up in the kitchen, having made him clean his own sick up first! Her easy mastery of the fundamentals of caring, put to best use with young children, or when she organised her friends to serve food at a wedding buffet with the line, 'You greet the guests, you're better at that stuff than I am.' I loved the fact that all the pictures of her travels are interspersed with images of children she encountered along the way. She seemed to manage to communicate with youngsters who couldn't have had much, if any, English.

I loved the fact that she existed, and blessed my life and many others with her fun and laughter. And I wouldn't have had it any other way. If I'd had the option to forego this grief by remaining childless, I wouldn't have taken it. And I'd have happily lived in a tent for the rest of my years if it would bring her back.

When someone said to me that they hoped 2017 would be better than 2016, it did jar a little . . . but I was now committed to just that. It's not that I expected to conquer grief, or that I'd get over Mia's death, because I just wouldn't. It was part of me and it would always overcome me at odd and uncomfortable moments. But life is a gift, and potentially all too transient, and we have a duty to our loved ones, alive and dead, to live it to the full. In honour of Mia, my resolution for 2017 was to reclaim my life.

12

Turnbull and Trump

Before Christmas 2016, I received a reply from my open letter to Malcolm Turnbull:

Dear Ms Ayliffe,

Thank you for your email dated 6 October 2016 regarding the need to improve regulation of working holiday (417) visa-holders who are working in regional Australia.

I want to start by offering my deepest condolences on the tragic loss of your daughter. I want to thank you for your genuine interest in protecting the well-being of other young backpackers visiting Australia. Working holidays encourage cultural exchange between and closer ties between Australia and participating countries and my government is strongly committed to deterring and penalising employers that exploit these workers.

Firstly, we have comprehensive work health and safety laws. Under these laws, employers have a duty to take all reasonably practicable steps to protect the health and safety of workers while at work. This includes ensuring that workers have been properly inducted to the worksite, have received adequate training to perform the job safely and supplied with the appropriate work safety equipment. An employer's responsibility to provide a safe workplace remains the same regardless of the workers' visa status.

From your correspondence it is unclear whether your daughter had access to employer-provided accommodation. However, in addition to ensuring a safe workplace, employers also have a duty to ensure the health and safety of those accessing employer-provided accommodation.

The Government is focused on increasing the understanding of and compliance with work health and safety laws by businesses and workers without compromising safety standards or imposing huge regulatory burden.

I understand your daughter had been working in Queensland. As such I have taken the liberty of forwarding your correspondence to Work Health and Safety Queensland (WHSQ), the relevant state authority with responsibility for workplace safety, so they can look further into this matter for you. Should you wish to contact WHSQ you can call them on 1300 362 128 or by visiting their website: www.worksafe.qld.gov.au.

Following concerns about exploitation of backpackers, Australia's workplace regulator – the fair work ombudsman – conducted an extensive two-year national enquiry into the experiences of backpackers working in Australia. The final report was released on 15 October 2016 and is available at: http://www.fairwork.gov.au.

A key part of the enquiry was a survey of more than 4000 overseas workers who have been granted a second-year 417 Visa after working in regional Australia. While many survey respondents were positive about their regional work experiences, the survey and other Inquiry work indicated serious concerns about the working conditions for backpackers, particularly while undertaking their 88 days of specified paid work. The regulator found that the 417 visa program adding to the vulnerability of visa-holders and creating an environment where, in some instances, visa-holders are subjected to unreasonable and unlawful demands by unscrupulous businesses and exploitative workforce cultures and behaviours have emerged in isolated and remote workplaces.

Intelligence gained throughout the enquiry has contributed to a number of enforcement actions taken against employers found to have exploited workers seeking a second-year 417 visa. The Government is greatly concerned by the cultural mindset of many employers hiring 417 visa-holders and we will continue working to ensure that 417 and other visa holders are not being exploited and are receiving their lawful entitlements while working in Australia.

We are delivering $20 million of additional funding for the Fair Work Ombudsman and strengthening its powers to deal with employers who exploit their workers. We will also introduce higher penalties for employers who exploit migrant workers and we have established a Migrant Workers' Taskforce to provide expert advice to the government on measures that would deliver better protections for overseas workers.

Once again please let me express my sincere sympathy on
the loss of your daughter and my gratitude for your interest in
protecting other young backpackers.

Yours sincerely,
Malcolm Turnbull

The letter was weighty, on quality, embossed paper, and initially
I was somewhat seduced into a feeling of excitement and pride.
I felt I had been vindicated to some extent for the effort I had
put in to campaigning, especially as Turnbull professed to recognise that there were issues with the 88 days program. However,
on a re-read, I came to the conclusion that I was being dismissed
summarily as an irritant, a nuisance, a grieving mother who had
just got everything out of proportion.

I later learnt that the money given to the Fair Work Ombudsman had been one of those ministerial sleights of hand where
money is given and retracted at the same time.

I responded to his reply with a letter suggesting that an ombudsman wasn't the answer, as a proactive response was required: people
who contacted an ombudsman generally did so from the comfort of
their own home when they didn't like the colour of their new sofa,
not when they were suffering from the effects of modern slavery.

Malcolm Turnbull didn't answer my second letter, and in fact
even despite repeated requests on my part for TV interviews in the
months to come, Turnbull refused to have any more to do with
me, likewise his ministers Steve Ciobo and Peter Dutton. This was
probably wise: I was Mia's mother so the moral high ground
was indubitably mine, but I was also right. Right about their broken
system being modern slavery. Still they did nothing to fix it.

As we entered the new year, Mary, Atessa and I, along with some volunteers from the local community, planned to run a Valentine's Ball fundraiser in the local town hall with lots of help from people in the community, auctioning off items local businesses had donated. We also commissioned a short publicity film about the aims of the campaign and began creating a website, www.88daysandcounting.com, which I envisaged as a TripAdvisor-style site aimed at directing young people towards good businesses, and away from the more insalubrious ones.

It was at this point that the profile of the campaign was given a massive lift from an unexpected quarter. It was February 2017, and I had spent the months since Mia's death in a state of permanent sobriety. Alcohol doesn't particularly agree with me. Although I can drink some wines and spirits and small amounts of beer, generally I go from sober to very ill within an hour or so, so I think I may have an intolerance (which Mia seemed to have inherited). Anyway, a good friend who was helping out with the masked ball invited Stewart and me up to their farm in the hills ostensibly to discuss plans for the ball, but also to get me drunk, as I think she'd decided that this would help me to cope. We duly headed up and had a nice meal together, then she offered me some Polish vodka. You live and learn, and I partook of the evil liquid.

The next day I was seriously unwell, to the extent I was bed-bound. I'd recently shot a short film to help publicise my campaign work, and as luck would have it, my contact there called with an urgent request to check the sound, as they needed to sign it off. I realised he needed it there and then, but I was so ill I couldn't even see the screen!

At 5 am the following morning, finally feeling well again, I opened my laptop to a message from the *Townsville Bulletin* asking me to comment on President Trump's inclusion of Mia's and Tom's deaths in a list of unreported terror incidents.

Confused, I checked the press, and there it was. The President of the United States had claimed that among other events on an arbitrary list, the reporting of Tom's and Mia's deaths was 'fake news' and that in fact it had been a terrorist incident.

It is certainly surreal – as someone who lives a quiet life in a tiny village in Derbyshire – to think that a person as high profile as Trump is paying attention to an aspect of your life. However, my life was spinning out of control anyway in terms of attention from the press, so I was less shocked by Trump's inclusion of Mia's and Tom's deaths in his list than affronted by it, since it was at best a crass and callous error. Our children's deaths were ugly and brutal, and must have been utterly terrifying, and I already found my mind attempting to recreate those events on a regular basis. This was a hurtful process, but I think it's something I needed to go through out of my love for Mia. One day I was going to find the strength to visit the place where she died and meet the man who sat with her, risking his own life through those long hours of her death, and held her hand to soothe her while she died in his arms.

If I could find the strength to do this, surely the White House could take the trouble to get their facts right? I realised that not only had attention not really been paid to the actual details of Mia's violent death, but that it probably had nothing at all to do with Trump himself; it was a poorly researched document produced by some underpaid official designed to suit the pernicious political agenda of his superior. And it was full of holes: every incident related to Islamic extremism was given maximum publicity, which was why Mia and Tom's deaths initially hit the headlines.

Sadly, the fact that a terrorist link had been ruled out from the out-set evidently hadn't registered in their scant and ineffectual research.

Tom's and Mia's deaths were not committed out of some mis-guided interpretation of the Koran. When I went to Australia to retrieve my daughter's body, I met the young man, Chris Porter, who accompanied Mia to Home Hill, and he pointed out that Ayad had not prayed in all the time they were together working in the fields, so he certainly showed no evidence of a fundamentalist adherence to Islam.

Attempts had already been made by right-wing Australian poli-tician Pauline Hanson to use Tom's and Mia's deaths as a means of preventing Muslim immigrants from entering Australia. But our children died at the hands of a French national. His name might suggest Islamic roots to some (he was of North African descent), but that's where the connection with Islam ends.

Trump had made a link between the deaths of our children and immigrants the world over. He was wrong about the Muslim terror threat, yet the connection was apt in one way: Mia had been disregarded and treated like a disposable commodity by the Australian government, who consider it fine for young people to be sent to the far reaches of their country in search of work and to run the gantlet of potential criminals through a system which they refuse to regulate, in much the same way as the needs of Syrian refugees are being overlooked as they are driven from one encampment to another, or the citizens of seven Middle-Eastern nations were being held in limbo in airports all over the US at this time.

I thought the UK press might want to know my take on this development. With a sense of deja vu, I honed an open letter to President Trump, and waited. That day I spoke to the *Mirror*, the

Guardian, the *Independent*, the *i*, Victoria Derbyshire of the BBC, Sky News, Channel 9 Australia, ABC America and CNN.

The open letter was also covered in the *Washington Post*, the *Daily Mail* and a number of other foreign news outlets whose existence I hadn't actually registered until that Tuesday. At any point I could have stopped and refused to speak to the press, but I decided I wanted to have my say.

An Open Letter to Mr Trump

The possibility of Mia's and Tom's deaths being consequent to an Islamic terror attack was discounted in the early stages of the police investigation through international collaboration on the parts of Queensland police department and the French anti-terrorist force. I have spoken to friends of Mia's and other backpackers who worked for long days in the fields with Ayad, and none of them ever saw him put down a prayer mat. *Salat* or prayer is the second of five pillars of Islam, and calls for five daily rituals of ablution, prayer and prostration. An Islamic fundamentalist by definition must respect the five pillars of Islam. It would be very hard to imagine someone managing to perform this ritual five times a day in the close confines of Home Hill Hostel without witnesses.

One of the reasons I took to blogging in the *Independent* newspaper was to discount this myth of a connection between my daughter's death and Islamic fundamentalism. Any fool can shout Allahu Akbar as they commit a crime. I have lived and worked in the Islamic world for a number of years, and wrote *The Rough Guide to Turkey*. Some of the research was carried out with Mia as a baby. Mia travelled in Turkey and Morocco too, albeit too briefly. We encountered nothing but respect and hospitality from people who are committed to courtesy and honouring their fellow human beings. This vilification of whole nation states and their people based on religion is a terrifying reminder of the horror that can ensue when we allow ourselves to be led by ignorant people into darkness and hatred.

My daughter's death will not be used to further this insane persecution of innocent people. The circumstances of Mia's and Tom's deaths prove that those with the strength of character to travel the world and learn about other cultures should be cherished as brave, resilient characters who have so much to offer if they are nurtured and given opportunities rather than defeated by adverse circumstances. Treating immigrants as disposable commodities and disregarding their safety causes deaths throughout our so-called civilised world, and my daughter was a victim of this disregard.

The reaction to the press coverage was overwhelming: 1.2 million impressions on Twitter in two days and countless people friending me and contacting me through Facebook Messenger. The vast majority of these contacts were supportive, and for a variety of reasons: Muslims who felt beleaguered and alone took my open letter as a sign of support in an ever more hostile world; Americans supported me in standing up to Trump and his attempt to twist the truth around my daughter's death; and huge numbers of immigrants and travellers felt vindicated by my stance on their plight. One I particularly loved and which energised me to carry on was this:

I met Mia in 2015 in Chefchaouen, Morocco. We spent almost a week together. I liked Mia immediately, she was fun and friendly but also generous and kind. I remember her talking to the locals: she didn't ignore the beggars, she played with the kids on the street and she fed as many stray cats as she could. I didn't find out what happened until today as I was still living in Morocco until recently. I am so shocked and sad, and so sorry for your loss. Mia talked about you a lot and I saw you were very close. I hope you're getting by.

I saw you on the news, and I just want to thank you so much. Using Mia's death to promote [Trump's] hatred of Muslims disgusts me. That man disgusts me and I think you are very brave for speaking up. My husband is Moroccan. He faces more and more problems from being Arabic. His family is Muslim and no one deserves the fear and hatred that they are facing. Thank you so so much. Again, I am so sorry. I will always remember Mia when I travel and try to share her open and adventurous spirit.

As is the way of the world, not everything I received was as positive. I've learnt to expect dissent as I know my views are not shared by everyone, and I have to say I welcome constructive criticism and the chance to enter into debate, even when it is spurious and fuelled by hatred. So I actually responded to people who I felt sincerely believed that ordinary Muslims were encouraged to abuse their own children or that they regularly cut off each other's hands.

I knew I would be accused of politicising Mia's and Tom's deaths. To my mind, though, their deaths *are* political.

*

I was convinced that the way forward was to make a documentary about the campaign, and I discussed this with Hugh Mann Adamson of Let There Be Light Productions in Sheffield, the company who had produced the short and filmed the Valentine's fundraiser. Being a Muslim of Pakistani descent, Hugh was so happy about my letter to Trump he said he would do anything he could to help further my cause, and had to be forced to take payment for the work he had done to date. We talked about the possibility of making a documentary together for free, but we both knew the time commitment and potential loss of earnings would be too great for him.

I knew I needed to look further afield for a potential film-maker, and speaking to friends in Australia I realised that from a campaign perspective my audience wasn't in the UK. It was the Australian public who needed to be convinced of the iniquities of the 88 days scheme.

Happily, the right person presented himself at the right time. My sister Ruth had travelled to Australia as a backpacker in her twenties, accompanied by an Australian called Tim Wilson. Tim was working in TV in Australia and had a number of contacts in news and current affairs programs. He contacted Jennifer Feller of *Australian Story* for me and immediately put us in touch.

What I really wanted was a film that looked at Mia's and Tom's deaths as a starting point, but then exposed the poor treatment of backpackers generally, asking questions about how the issues could be resolved. If possible, I wanted to be low key or not on camera at all. Ideally I would feed information and potential interviewees to a journalist who would appear on screen. That isn't *Australian Story*'s format, however, and I soon discovered the focus would all be on me.

As with all decisions, I ran the idea of the documentary past Mia, who now represented my conscience. She warned me to be careful, and to check at each juncture that this was about progressing the campaign. Otherwise, I got the green light.

13

Australian Story

AGREEING TO HAVE A DOCUMENTARY MADE ABOUT YOU FEELS LIKE the ultimate in narcissism! The process resembles staring into a two-way mirror, knowing that on the other side is a huge and potentially hostile audience, who is analysing your face for wrinkles and blemishes, criticising your ticks and mannerisms, and wondering why you're staring into the mirror at all!

At the beginning of the process I was extremely wary as I didn't know how I would be portrayed. In February and March 2017 I had a few weeks of inactivity – I wasn't allowed by the ABC to do any press work and the campaign website was still in its infancy, so I couldn't work on that yet either. During this period I no longer felt like a campaigner – I felt deflated and unsure of the path I was taking, and my morale had dropped to rock bottom. The idea of going to Australia and trying to make an impact on what was only my second visit was quite terrifying, especially since I would be followed by a film crew. What had I let myself in for?

The idea was to make a two-part documentary. The first part would be filmed in Derbyshire, to show the audience where Mia grew up and about our lives. I had arranged to meet a returnee backpacker that the ABC would shoot, and was also to be filmed being interviewed by well-known radio presenter Jeremy Vine for his popular afternoon chat show.

The second part was more of an unknown quantity, and in fact neither producer Jennifer Feller nor I had any idea of whether we would have enough material for it. I had a vague plan about visiting regions that were trouble spots, and I wanted to meet members of parliament and the UK's High Commissioner to Australia, but whether anyone would agree to meet me was a different matter.

In terms of the campaign, I knew it was an opportunity I couldn't miss. This was a chance to get a huge level of press attention, which I was eager to harness in order to call for change that would have a tangible impact on thousands of backpackers working in agricultural, mining, fishing or construction jobs in regional Australia. It was my passport to trade ideas with any number of campaigners in Australia – Alison Rahill of the Salvation Army's Freedom Partnership, the unions, representatives for Pacific Islanders (who often undertake horticultural work), faith groups, MPs and former slaves. Pacific Islanders are a particularly vulnerable group of workers in Australia. The Seasonal Worker Programme seems better conceived than the 88 days program, in that all workers are given a period of induction and assigned to workplaces and accommodation that should be compliant with legislation. However, the visa bonds them to a particular employer, and culturally they are unlikely to make complaints, as they are often working to send money home rather than for permission to stay a second year.

As the main participants on the Seasonal Worker Programme, Pacific Islanders often seem to be exposed to the same poor living conditions and low piece rates as workers on the 88 days. To date, fourteen workers have died on the program, and while some of the deaths were due to traffic accidents, others are more perturbing, with advocates suggesting that poor diet and unacceptable working conditions may be contributing factors.

Most importantly it was my ticket in to Parliament House in Canberra to meet crucial figures in the campaign against modern slavery, including the UK Independent Anti-Slavery Commissioner Kevin Hyland, who was due to appear at an inquiry into establishing a Modern Slavery Act in Australia. Kevin was now firmly ensconced as a hero in my eyes. He had fought for the rights of migrant workers in the UK both during his career as a police officer and later as the UK's Anti-Slavery Commissioner. As the first incumbent of that role he had helped to define it, and he set the bar high. He had made connections with campaigners all over the world, and had improved the working conditions of countless people whose lives would otherwise have been tainted by the misery of slave-like conditions including imprisonment and child prostitution.

So how did it feel being filmed? To be honest, I felt completely exposed with this level of scrutiny and, at the same time, unworthy of the attention. In reality, most of it is incredibly tedious. You work long and hard, repeating the same action over and over until you get it right. *Australian Story* is a different format to other documentaries I'd watched, in that the subject is also the narrator. This meant having to answer questions in complete sentences, which is counterintuitive until you get the hang of it.

Jennifer had spent many hours on the phone with me before she arrived in the UK, so we both knew what to expect and where the narrative was heading, at least with the first episode. But nothing prepared me for this wiry dynamo of a woman or her offhand charm. This first encounter was tense, to say the least. I met Jennifer at the train station and we walked slowly up through the village while she took a call from her cameraman and enthused to him about how perfectly picturesque our village is, and how it would make a great backdrop for the story. 'How lucky I live somewhere so quaint,' I thought drily. At home I made a coffee to Jennifer's specifications (a skinny decaf) and we talked about the situation for backpackers in Australia. Jennifer, laughing, suddenly came out with, 'But how do you expect the Australian government to regulate this system? It's a big country, you know, and some of the places these young people work are incredibly remote. I mean, Home Hill, it's in the middle of nowhere!' The fact that she was laughing when she said this made me see red and I turned on her in a complete fury.

'If you can't regulate the system, why are you expecting our kids to participate in it? Don't you think I know they're working in remote locations, with absolutely no training? If Mia hadn't been killed by Ayad, it could have been any number of other things which would have killed her. The heat . . . a snake, according to her she had no induction whatsoever!'

Honestly, at that point I was ready to draw a line under the whole project. She just didn't seem to get the scale of the problem, how dangerous it was for young backpackers, or how her government was responsible for the welfare of participants. However, I think Jennifer could persuade anyone in the world into doing what she wanted of them, because of her diffidence, an endearing candidness, and an enduring expectation that she will get what she wants, however long it takes!

She had earmarked certain people she wanted to interview and made it clear what kind of things she would be looking for in terms of visuals. I also spent a long time talking to Alison Rahill, who would be instrumental in planning the Australian-set episode, from Home Hill to Bundaberg. Without Alison and the Freedom Partnership, the second episode would never have happened.

As it transpired I needn't have worried about how I was to be portrayed. Jennifer was an experienced professional and guided me through the whole process. The first episode was really about engaging the audience in the emotional side of the campaign, a fairly straightforward task. I showed her around Cromford, including the bookshop where Mia used to spend a lot of time as a child reading on the floor of the kids section, and the bookshop cafe she worked in as a teenager.

The following day she returned with cameraman Niall in tow and then began a gruelling three days for everyone. I gave a three-hour interview in our living room about Mia and our relationship, which left me drained and also nearly finished off Niall's camera battery. He'd never worked for *Australian Story* before so was unaware of how much power he'd need to complete the day.

Mia's friend Ro Horton turned up, and was interviewed, and then it was Stewart's turn. That evening news editor Rachael Gilchrist arrived from her workplace at the BBC studios in Derby. She was planning to come to Australia with me for the second part of the journey in order to put together some coverage, which she was hoping would be broadcast nationally. We had an evening meal together, but by this stage we were all exhausted.

The following day Jennifer and I squeezed into the spaces around the camera equipment in Niall's hire car for more of the same with Les and Sandra Jackson. This interview had been organised by Jennifer and it was good to catch up with them, however briefly. They spoke about some of the issues Tom had experienced on his 88 days, including his claim that his passport was retained by one hostel owner, which he told them about in a phone call.

That night Jennifer, myself and Niall all drove to London – three adults squashed in among all the equipment – and arrived at 3 am.

Prior to Jennifer's approach to take part in *Australian Story*, I had been contacted by the Jeremy Vine show, and was told that Vine had heard me speaking on *Woman's Hour* and wanted to interview me on his own radio show. I only realised how big a deal this was when Stewart informed me of Vine's enormous following. Vine is the equivalent of a shock jock, and has a huge daily lunchtime audience across the UK for his current affairs program. Jennifer was keen to film the interview. There followed some negotiations around health and safety between the two sets of technicians, but Vine was keen to accommodate the TV cameras as he appreciated the import of the campaign.

The night before I stayed with a friend who lived near the BBC studios, while Jennifer stayed in a hotel, so we agreed on a time to meet beforehand. En route to the studios, I nipped in to the ladies in a pub to apply some make-up. I met Jennifer at the agreed time and when I told her what I'd been doing she looked at me quizzically.

'Make-up? But it's a radio show?'

'Yes, but you're filming me, Jennifer!'

'Oh yes, so we are!'

I was incredibly nervous, being filmed, potentially making a fool of myself live on air, and I had to take deep breaths and connect with Mia's spirit and the purpose of the campaign just to step foot over the threshold. I needn't have worried. Vine was incredibly sympathetic, loved my interview and helped to drive the point home about the 88 days. Later he told me he had a nephew travelling in Australia who was weighing up whether to embark on the 88-day program, so it was personal to him. The response from his audience was gratifying too, as people called to speak about some negative experiences, reinforcing my point beautifully. One caller said he'd had a lovely time doing his farm work, but Vine pointed out this didn't disprove anything, and he was right. People *can* have good experiences, and there *are* good farmers involved in the scheme. I've never disputed that fact and I try to start every interview by acknowledging the great people working in that space.

The following day was spent interviewing further London-based friends of mine and Mia's, while trying to get hold of a backpacker, Tom Webb, who we were intending to interview about his aborted attempt at completing the 88 days. His story had arrived some months previously, and it had moved me to write to his local MP to see if she could get him any help.

Tom wrote to tell me about his experiences of undertaking farm work in order to spend another year in Australia. Initially he got on well working on piece rates but was earning very little, just enough to cover his rent and some food. When he was promoted to the packing shed he was delighted, because it meant he was on award rates and he didn't mind the lifting work as he was used to it from his experiences in the construction industry back home. He described giving 100 per cent to the work and he enjoyed it so much he volunteered to work in the busiest part of the packing factory as it helped to make the time go faster. Things were going well and the supervisors were friendly towards him until one day he had to get a pallet off a stack. The pallets were not always in good condition and as he pulled the pallet a plank of wood ripped off. The pallet fell on both of his legs, causing a lot of pain. At least one of the supervisors witnessed this accident, but did not check to see if Tom was okay.

Tom carried on working, possibly in shock, because it was so busy in his section and his colleagues would have struggled without him. He pointed out to me that the culture was one in which you'd be fired if you complained about anything.

During the weekend the injury got worse and became very painful. When Tom arrived back at work on Monday he let his bosses know he was in pain and asked to take it easy for a few days as he still wanted to work. The supervisor in charge refused him permission, saying this would be unfair on the others. Shocked by this, Tom carried on as he feared losing his job.

Later that day at lunch Tom went to stand up from the table and there was a loud snapping noise which everyone in the vicinity heard. It was so painful he could hardly walk. The supervisor suggested he go to the doctor's and get it looked at. He was shocked to discover he was basically expected to find his own way to hospital. He went to the doctor's but only had enough money to get it looked at, not enough to pay for treatment or scans. All he could do was buy antibiotics, as one of the cuts on his knee was infected.

Tom took a few days off but was worried he would be fired if he didn't return, so he went back to work. He was really struggling to walk and as the nature of his role meant he was frequently moving, he was in agony.

One of the permanent Australian workers realised Tom was injured and asked how it happened, and seemed shocked by Tom's reply. She took Tom to the canteen to sit and wait for the health and safety officer. Tom was then asked about the situation and the officer seemed concerned at first. He was taken to the doctor's then to the hospital for a scan on his legs. They had to wait a few days for the results, and Tom was given light duties in the packing shed. After a week or so the doctor gave him the all-clear that nothing was broken. He was still in a lot of pain but nothing else was done about the matter.

Tom tried to get on with working as he needed to get his 88 days finished. But then he received the bad news that he had been fired. He returned home to the UK, still in pain and with his 88 days incomplete.

I managed to track Tom down eventually and interview him in Camden, London. Jennifer agreed with me that Tom was convincing, and had had a raw deal in Australia. She left with more than enough for one episode, and there followed a wait of two weeks while she went into furious editing mode. Neither of us had any idea of what would happen when I got to Australia, or even whether the material would stretch to two episodes. We didn't know whether we would be allowed to film at Home Hill Backpackers, whether I'd gain access even, whether I'd manage to meet and talk to backpackers, farmers, politicians or other stakeholders . . . I had no idea what to expect. But one thing was certain: I was going to give it my best shot.

Before I arrived in Australia, I received some good news. Billy Bragg had been performing in a small venue in Coffs Harbour in front of a crowd that included backpackers on their 88 days, so the ABC approached to ask if they could interview him about our friendship and use the footage in *Australian Story*. Billy agreed, and Jennifer was pleased with the footage, so at least we had one single scene – and an endorsement of the campaign – to use for the second part.

This journey to Australia was far less fraught than the previous one. Rachael Gilchrist, the Radio Derby journalist, was a seasoned traveller, and insisted we needed a hotel at Heathrow airport to cope with the early start the following morning. It had never occurred to me to do this, but it's a procedure I now adhere to religiously because it mitigates a lot of the stress of the journey. It meant we could have a drink and a chat the night before, and although the flight was punishingly early, we managed to have a decent trip. I caught up on the schedule we would be following, and we both read and slept, knowing we would be filmed on touchdown.

On arrival, sure enough Jennifer and Alison Rahill were waiting with a camera crew. Tired as I was I went through the various manoeuvres required for them to extract the perfect fifteen seconds denoting 'Rosie's arrival in Australia'! It was gruelling, but by now I was used to these repetitive actions, and I was starting to realise how impactful the documentary could be if we got it right.

The first night in Australia was such a relief. With the long journey out of the way, Alison, Jennifer, Rachael and I went for a meal in a quiet, simple restaurant. Though Alison and I had already had a few Skype calls, I don't think they prepared me for the warmth of her welcome and her huge personality. Alison really is like no one else I've ever met, at once incredibly reassuring to be around, and a powerful force in the modern slavery movement. I have so much admiration for her and her husband Matt Pulford. To me they are the true face of Australia, both humane, full of a lightness and good humour, but also highly effective practitioners.

The combination of Rachael, Alison and Jennifer was a good one, as they were all professional and reassuring, and I began to have faith that with their influence, I could have enough of an impact to improve the 88 days scheme: I really started to believe I was going to make a success of both the trip and the campaign. I felt like things were falling into place, and that people I needed would come to me at the right times. I had a strong sense that people wanted change in Australia, and I could be the instrument to help effect that change. The real work was being done behind the scenes by people like Professor Anthony Forsyth, the National Union of Workers (NUW) and Alison and her colleagues at the Freedom Partnership. But if the press was interested in my story, then I was going to strike while the proverbial iron was fresh out of the conflagration that was the carnage at Home Hill.

Rachael and I spent the first day together sightseeing in Sydney and getting to know each other. I was glad of the company as I was affected deeply by being back on Australian soil. I felt Mia's presence everywhere, which was both lovely and a huge shock. I knew she would have walked these pavements, admired these views and eaten in these restaurants, and I kept thinking I saw glimpses of her from the corner of my eye.

One of the first things I did was to close Mia's Australian bank account in order to obtain her bank statements, which meant I was able to discover all the places she visited. Her final transaction was for flowers and a bottle of prosecco for my birthday, which cost her $120. She always bought me beautiful presents.

Rachael and I got on a ferry – the wrong one as it happened – and had a tour of the harbour. Eventually we ended up in a restaurant where we met Alison and her husband Matt for another wonderful meal, this time seafood with a view of Sydney Opera House. If I wasn't so emotionally drained it would have been magical, but I was in the company of compassionate, wonderful people and they made all the difference, as they recognised how traumatic this trip was for me.

We flew to Townsville and hired a car. The visit to Shelley's Backpackers in Home Hill (also known as the Home Hill Backpackers) was shaping up to be a disaster. I felt like I was losing control of my purpose in visiting the hostel in the first place. I had wanted to walk in, introduce myself to Shelley and try to understand her take on that night, but because I'd had to inform her that I was coming, and with a film crew, she refused to speak to me or even be in the same space. Instead, she sent her loss adjuster to meet us. The whole purpose of my visit had therefore been negated because of the requirements of the press. This was frustrating.

I knew any decent chance of press coverage relied on having footage of me meeting Shelley. There was no way the BBC or the ABC would cover my story in the kind of detail I wanted without visiting the hostel. At one point it looked as if it might not happen, at least for the BBC: the loss adjuster wouldn't let me in to the hostel until Monday morning. Rachael had booked a flight back on the Tuesday to Sydney, and was counting on the footage.

Understandably, Rachael was worried that her journey all the way from the UK might be for nothing; so much so that at one point I agreed to walk in to the hostel miked up, and just visit the bathroom and leave, in order to film a few seconds of footage. I messaged Daniel Richards, the young man who was with Mia when she died. We discussed the layout and workings of the hostel and he said it was entirely feasible for me to pull this off, as Shelley wasn't around the premises that often anyway. On reflection, I decided against it. Though I was confident that the ABC would produce a high-quality documentary that could help the campaign, I had to be mindful of how I would be portrayed elsewhere in the media if it got out that I had trespassed. The one word that had been used to describe my behaviour – by press and followers alike – was dignified, and I didn't want to give way to a careless impulse and destroy that reputation. There was too much riding on it.

When the respective journalists thought through the options, it became clear that there were sensible ways around the issue. This was mainly because Rachael's footage was for radio, so she didn't need visual recordings. Instead we recorded her questions in situ, and then after the visit Jennifer would ask me the questions again and record my response.

Ray Rohweder (Queensland Police Department's regional crime co-ordinator), Nick Bach (the arresting officer), Kelly Harvey (the inspector in charge of the case) and I met the loss adjuster on the balcony of Home Hill Hostel. I presume the loss adjuster was there to try to minimise publicity around the deaths of Tom and Mia, so I wondered whether an insurance claim had been made around loss of earnings subsequent to the deaths. No cameras were allowed, but I made a transcript from memory straight after the interview. One of the things that was most apparent was the bravery of Daniel Richards in staying with Mia and trying to save her life.

It was confirmed that Mia had not been unconscious after the first blow, as I had first been led to believe. On receiving the fatal wound to her heart, she had run for safety and hidden in the bathroom, which is where Daniel found her. Daniel had called for Tom, but Ayad had swan-dived off the balcony and – not realising what had happened – Tom went to check on Ayad first. It later transpired that Ayad had broken a vertebra in his neck when he fell to the ground.

Daniel was still shouting for Tom, and so Tom headed up to the bathroom. At this point Ayad came back up the stairs and forced open the door of the bathroom, inflicting fatal blows to Tom.

Daniel saw all of this as Mia lay dying in his arms. He has no idea why his life was spared. Apparently when the paramedics arrived Tom was a bloody mess, with wounds to his head and eye, so they assumed he was already dead. Instead they tried to revive Mia first, because there was no blood on her anywhere. But she was already beyond help.

Meanwhile Shelley's son-in-law and Shelley arrived at the scene, but they left the premises promptly to call the police, and several backpackers found themselves left in the hostel's grounds with the killer.

After his arrest, Ayad attacked two police officers, and during his detainment he was said to have attacked a total of twelve officers, so he was made to wear a helmet as he was taken to the cells, and was later considered too dangerous to appear in person in court, and instead questioned via a video link-up.

After I'd had all this explained to me, on the spot where Mia received her fatal wounds, I went to the toilet and sat in a cubicle. I was devastated from having to relive Mia's last moments blow by blow, and I wept as I sat there, feeling Mia's anguish as she lay dying. I thought about the description of that night I'd just had relayed to me. I wasn't surprised that she had fought for her life, because she was so feisty, and also loved the life she was living so much. But the distance she had travelled after receiving that fatal wound! Her body had allowed her to make that journey. Somehow in that moment I reverted to the faith of my childhood, and I said the Lord's Prayer. 'Forgive us our trespasses, as we forgive those who trespass against us.' I knew that even though I would continue to argue for systemic change, I would simultaneously follow the path of forgiveness, because that was how I had been brought up, and it was at the core of everything Mia had believed in.

Afterwards Jennifer interviewed me and I remember expressing my amazement that Mia had come into the world as clean as a pin and gone out the same way. I sobbed convulsively for most of the interview, but I knew she needed that footage, and had new impetus to expose this pernicious system even more than before.

We headed to a local bar after the filming. I think we all needed a drink. As we were ordering I noticed an elderly guy trying to catch my attention. He obviously knew who I was. He introduced himself as Arthur and told me that he'd known Tom quite well as they were both Liverpool supporters and had bonded over shared memories and pints.

Arthur told us that he'd met two young women who said they'd heard about backpackers being asked for sexual favours out in the field and farmers refusing to sign their paperwork if they didn't comply.

Arthur said he could barely believe his ears, so he went to speak to a local farming family whom he trusted. He asked them whether they'd heard similar stories and they confirmed that this practice was not a one-off in that area.

As Arthur was speaking Jennifer had taken out her phone to record his comments, but she needn't have as he agreed to speak on camera and we recorded him saying exactly the same thing for *Australian Story*. Given this was our first day of filming we began to feel optimistic that things were going to fall into place.

The following day we met one of Mia's former employers out at her farm. I remember Mia talking about her in one of our last phone conversations before she died. Mia felt she was kind and might be able to sign off her days, as she had helped other backpackers in the same circumstances. What Mia didn't tell me was that, according to her former employer, she'd confided her fears regarding Ayad. Afterwards, Mia's former employer described to me how Mia had jumped out of a vehicle and run over to give her a hug, and afterwards told her about her fears of Ayad. Remembering that Mia had told me that this woman might be a possible source of 'rescue' from the 88 days, I think Mia was hoping that she would take her in and give her refuge. Mia hugged her in order to try to awaken a maternal instinct to protect. This was entirely Mia's way: she read people, and acted accordingly.

The thought that Mia's last few days had been so fearful was something I needed time to assimilate. If true, this was devastating news – incredibly painful to learn about.

The woman was sweet, caring and maternal in her demeanour, and I could easily imagine Mia getting out of the car and giving her a hug one morning, as she described.

Later, the coroner did not find there was sufficient evidence that Mia made any disclosure to her former employer about being harassed by Ayad as Mia didn't confide this to anyone else. However, to my mind this was exactly in keeping with Mia's 'modus operandi'. She always played her cards close to her chest, even when she was a little girl, and she would often only tell me after she had worked a problem out what had happened and what she'd done to solve it. She abhorred baseless gossip, but if she couldn't solve something herself she would confide in the person she thought could solve the problem, and that person only.

Once I'd said goodbye, we made a return visit to Home Hill, this time with some beautiful plants and a weighty stone statue of the Buddha, which we used to create a little memorial garden for Mia and Tom. I asked permission first from Ray Rohweder, and I chose the plants carefully. I felt this was a positive thing to do, and some Italian backpackers came out to chat and to help me. They had received very little work since arriving, and one of them was almost destitute and being threatened with eviction. Later that afternoon I was making the finishing touches to the memorial when I met three Finnish girls, who I chatted with about how they were finding things at the hostel. They too were suffering from not having received any work, and I asked out of curiosity whether anyone had arrived after them and been prioritised for work. 'Yes, a Georgian girl.'

'Excuse me for asking, but what did she look like?' The three girls I was talking to were quite plain, and possibly approaching their thirties, so nearing the top end of the age range for the 88 days program.

'She was beautiful, so vivacious and fun, and just nineteen years old.'

*

Once we'd finished filming at Home Hill we made the long journey down to Bundaberg. Owing to legal limits and timings, we broke the drive at Rockhampton, where I was filmed having a conversation over Skype with Stewart. I was struggling without his calming influence by this stage, and it was really good to make contact and hear about what was happening back home.

I was near to the edge with exhaustion. I felt as if I had no privacy and every second of my time was being imposed on. But I reminded myself that I was in Australia for a reason, and could already tell that this episode was going to have an impact.

The next day the film crew weren't allowed to get on the road early as they'd been filming until around 10 pm the night before, but I decided on impulse to escape, and so I left Rockhampton in my own hire car as soon as I awoke around dawn. I needed some headspace to think about everything I had learnt, and maybe three hours alone on the road would do me some good. Besides, I still wanted to make Alison Rahill's morning meeting in Bundaberg, which Jennifer had decided last-minute to cut from the filming schedule.

I arrived at the Salvation Army's lovely sanctuary in a state of near exhaustion, but was delighted and reinvigorated when I met some of the workers, including Aunty Jane, who was a second-generation slave, and reminded me so much of Annie, my maternal grandmother. I also met Moe Turaga for the first time and heard his heartbreaking story of arriving in Australia from Fiji to find that working conditions were far from what he had been led to expect. (Moe later told Alison that he was inspired to tell his own story because I had spoken about what happened to Mia, and about the campaign.)

Moe was invited over to work in Australia by his cousin. While working in the agriculture sector, Moe and his fellow Fijian workers were informed by the cousin that the lion's share of their wages was being sent home to family, but in fact this wasn't happening, they were just being grossly underpaid. Some were so hungry they ended up stealing and slaughtering a cow in order to survive. Eventually someone at Moe's local church asked him some carefully worded questions and discovered the truth about his plight, and he was rescued by the Salvation Army. He and his colleagues had basically been subjected to a brutalising regime which could only be described as modern slavery.

I felt at home among the Pacific Islanders and identified with their plight. These lovely, open-hearted folk felt like my people.

Jennifer picked me up from the Salvation Army building and we headed out for my second meeting of the day, which was on farmer and campaigner Allan Mahoney's beautiful mango farm. When we arrived, everyone was sitting in a circle looking uncomfortable and not talking to each other, but as soon as I walked in everyone seemed to relax. Moe and I hugged and I noticed Allan had some quite impressive body art, so we all started comparing our tattoos, and everyone became a lot more relaxed and chatty. Jennifer looked on, and later told me she really regretted not having a cameraman to hand to film this moment of spontaneous connection.

Allan had lost a child himself, and was therefore highly empathic, not only to me but also to the backpackers he encountered from running his farming business, and he was well aware of the iniquities in the system. He had visited working hostels in the notorious Bundaberg region and come to the conclusion that a percentage of them should be closed down immediately. He differed from me in terms of solutions, though: he thought the solution to the numerous and entwined problems of the 88 days scheme was squarely on the shoulders of contractors and working hostels, and he was against further regulation, which he considered red tape. While I sympathised with that view, I did think the program had been imposed by the federal government, and therefore should either be abolished by them or properly regulated.

That evening, we managed to fit in an interview with a back-packer who had experienced poor conditions and been lied to about work. Djuro was a cancer-survivor, and a thoughtful and philo-sophical individual who seemed to ooze credibility and integrity, perhaps because of his backstory: his father was a Bosnian who had been killed in the troubles in former Yugoslavia, so his mother emigrated with Djuro to Denmark. He first contacted me having seen with his own eyes what was happening in the fields of Queensland, telling me he thought backpackers needed to protest against the conditions in a mass rally. Later, when he had completed his days, he and his girlfriend went to stay with Alison. Alison and Matt's position was that they considered the couple to be traumatised. Both Djuro and his girlfriend had times when they broke down in tears, their morale was so low. Djuro likened his mental state to that of a survivor of abuse who had been degraded and no longer trusted his own judgement regarding his worth in society.

There was more to come. The following day, having barely slept, I met Grace Grace, Queensland's minister for agriculture, on a potato farm where we were filmed talking about the issues and the solutions that were currently on the table. I made the point that I thought enforcement was a key aspect of the solution. Without a body akin to the UK's Gangmasters and Labour Abuse Authority, whose officers now have the power to arrest traffickers and abusive contractors, I saw little hope of lasting change in the Australian industry. I also knew that other activists wanted to see the introduction of an industry-wide manslaughter charge for negligence, as in their view the fines clearly weren't enough of a disincentive: there were too many debilitating injuries and fatal accidents within the agricultural, mining and construction sectors, although, conveniently for the Turnbull administration, without registration in the 88 days system, it was impossible to tell how many of these were backpacker-related.

From Bundaberg we flew down to Melbourne, where I had my first encounter with members of the National Union of Workers, who were striving to recruit backpackers in order to give them all the protection they could offer. The union was making some headway, but I think it was proving an uphill battle to persuade companies to allow them to organise workers on their premises. The unions were fully aware of the issues facing migrant workers and had substantial data to back this up. They provided swathes of case studies to Professor Anthony Forsyth regarding underpayment of migrant workers, including backpackers in the state of Victoria, and they also provided a number of case studies to the *Four Corners* documentary 'Slaving Away', featuring Taiwanese and Chinese workers and their exploitation in Australia's food industry. One of the union workers, Sherry Huang, persuaded a rape victim to give a powerful testimony on camera, plus extensive information about abuse among the Taiwanese community. She forwarded me a number of examples, including pictures of the mangled hand of a young worker whose former career as a plumber in Taiwan would now be over. He received £60,000 in compensation.

The other meeting in Melbourne was with a Canadian called Chelsey, an amazing young woman who told her story to camera. She described her attempted rape on a farm, and subsequent treatment by both the police and the contractor connected to her working hostel. Chelsey's attacker was the owner of a farm in Victoria. Chelsey says he gave her a tablet which she swallowed. She thinks it may have been a date-rape drug as it made her drowsy. She fought him off to the extent that both of them were covered in scratches and bruises.

However, when Chelsey reported the attack, the police said there was 'not enough evidence' and failed to offer Chelsey a forensic examination or any form of support or counselling. They told her that her attacker would be interviewed that evening, but she saw him in a local bar later that day, and was told he spent the entire evening there with no visit from the police. Later, I was reliably informed that the police had refused to interview Chelsey because 'there had been drugs involved' – i.e. Chelsey had taken the tablet offered to her. My informant also told me that the federal police had been less than impressed with this dereliction of duty on the part of the state police, as an opportunity to convict Chelsey's assailant had been thrown away.

The following year, the would-be rapist went on to attack again, but this time the attempt was interrupted when his mother arrived at the family home. He appeared in court while we were still filming *Australian Story*, but since he pleaded guilty Chelsey was not called as a witness. He was given a community service order and was not put on the sex offenders register. I found it shocking that a serial attacker could possibly still work with backpackers.

Moreover, the day after Chelsey reported the attack, the contractor working with the hostel concerned gave everyone in

the hostel work except Chelsey, which she took to be a deliber-
ate punishment for her decision to go to the police. He also sent
another young woman to work with the attacker.

Chelsey recounted all of this with impressive poise and dignity. She decided in the end to be filmed incognito because, as she
pointed out, it didn't matter who she was, it could have happened
to anyone. I'm not so sure that just anyone would have had the
strength to fight the guy off, or the integrity to speak to the media
subsequent to the attack, but like all the Canadian women I have
met through my campaign, Chelsey is a force to be reckoned with,
and highly attuned to human rights issues.

I managed to catch up with Chelsey and her partner later that
day for dinner, and was again impressed by her calmness and self-
sufficient manner. I asked her if she'd had any counselling and she
replied that she didn't think it was necessary – she had fought off
her attacker and escaped, and because of this she felt empowered
by the experience. Her sole purpose in speaking out was to alert
others to the dangers of the 88 days, and of that particular set-up.
Too many young people are intimidated from going to the police
and reporting transgressions by the threats delivered to them by
their abusers. Backpackers in these awful situations feel vulnerable
in a foreign land, and fear farmers will take them to court for libel,
or even have them deported.

One of the best moments of my trip was meeting the British High
Commissioner to Australia in her sumptuous house in Canberra.
Her Excellency Menna Rawlings is incredibly gracious, but also
down-to-earth, and she was so galvanised by my idea that the
consulates should meet to discuss joint action that she offered to

call her German counterpart straight away, but we were both due in parliament within the hour. I was on a gruelling schedule!

This was for a hearing of the Inquiry into Establishing a Modern Slavery Act in Australia, chaired by MP Chris Crewther, which was also attended by Kevin Hyland, the UK's Anti-Slavery Commissioner. I had met Kevin the night before to explain the problematic aspects of the current 88 days program. I was only an onlooker while the MPs discussed the anti-slavery agenda, but I think some members of the press assumed I addressed the committee. Members of parliament kindly took me for lunch once the session was over, and I used this opportunity to raise some of the issues there.

Senator Linda Reynolds asked for more information on the campaign, so I offered to send this when I got back to Derbyshire. After my return to the UK I put together a report from all the sources I could find, including a report by the academic Dr Elsa Underhill of Deakin University in which she examines work safety issues of temporary workers employed in Victoria, and Professor Forsyth's report on infringements of backpackers' rights in Victoria, together with first-hand accounts of backpackers and an account of my own findings and recommendations. Gratifyingly, Senator Reynolds asked if she could put this to the committee of the Inquiry into Establishing a Modern Slavery Act in Australia.

The *Australian Story* trip finished off with a second visit to Mia's beloved Byron Bay. There I met Daniel Richards for the first time, and caught up with Chris Porter and an old friend of mine, Jayne. Although there was filming to be done, that evening Jayne and I managed to get time alone with Daniel. This brave, wiry Welshman is a strong character with a fragile heart. He can be incredibly funny, and has a sensitive and caring side, as evidenced by his care of Mia in her final hours, for which I will always love and cherish him.

Jayne is a trained counsellor and was impressed by Daniel's resilience in the face of what he had lived through at Home Hill. We spent the evening getting to know each other, and I think Jayne and I both felt concerned for Daniel, but pretty sure he would pull through. It was just nine months since the attack, so understandably he was still having horrible flashbacks and would often feel isolated by the experience, with nobody to talk to on the backpacker scene who really understood the horrors of that night. I think having the time together and just being able to talk about everything, and to reminisce about Mia and Tom was important for all of us. At last I could convey personally the gratitude I felt for Daniel's bravery.

At the end of this hectic and demanding trip I returned to Sydney for a few days. Jesse, Mia's friend from Surfers, joined me. These past few weeks took their toll, and I was laid low by the worst migraine I've ever had. She ended up looking after me, and was incredibly supportive, but it wasn't what we'd expected to happen and I was disappointed that I didn't have more to give. Jesse was still grieving deeply, and I hadn't been able to help her at all.

14

Going to Air

AUSTRALIAN STORY: LONG WAY FROM HOME AIRED ON 10 AND 17 JULY 2017. To my mind, the second episode was far more impactful than the first, as I think many Australian viewers were being confronted with the realities of the 88 days scheme for the first time. I hoped that seeing those realities through the eyes of a parent who had suffered such a terrible loss would spur people into joining me in calling for changes to the system.

Stewart met me in Australia with the plan that once we'd dealt with the publicity, we would have some time together exploring the country, which I was beginning to recognise as both beautiful and fascinating. We planned an itinerary starting in Sydney and then flying to Cairns, with a visit to the rainforest, then back down to Brisbane to catch up with Jesse and her partner Rylea on the Gold Coast. We wanted to see something of the country and just enjoy a holiday without having to face any of the horrors of the previous year.

Unfortunately, TV works to a very different schedule and needed me to hit the ground running. We were met off the flight by an ABC cameraman, who took us to the studio where I did a photoshoot. The resultant pictures are probably the worst I'd ever had taken, despite a prolonged make-over and a professional cameraman, who really did his best!

The next day was even tougher. Stewart and I met Jennifer early at the ABC studios, and after grabbing a bite to eat were taken up to the *News Breakfast* studio. Jennifer and I talked at length prior to the interview, and I think I delivered it really well, so much so that the interviewer came over afterwards to congratulate me on how well it had gone. I remembered to ask why the Tourism Minister Steven Ciobo was spending $10 million promoting the working holiday visa program when he could be using the money more wisely for reform, and I asked Minister for Home Affairs Peter Dutton to meet me and explain the state the program was in, and what he intended to do to reform it.

During the course of that day I gave thirteen separate press interviews, which took from breakfast at 8 am until around 6 pm, and in all of them I professed my willingness to meet Peter Dutton. I don't think Stewart realised quite how hard I worked as a campaigner until he witnessed this, but he later said he was exhausted just watching it. I felt elated to be given the chance to explain the campaign to a wider audience, and I think an excess of adrenaline saw me through that day, as it had through most of the filming of *Australian Story*.

Jennifer was really pleased with the interviews, but we were all unprepared for what was to happen next. As Stewart and I slipped away for a couple of days' sightseeing around Sydney, all hell was breaking loose in the ABC studios, with people calling and writing in from all corners of Australia. *Australian Story* staff said they'd never had a response like it.

Stewart and I made a decision to stick to our previous plan. I really thought I'd done the campaign justice that day in the ABC studios, and a work-life balance is just as important when you're campaigning as it is in everyday life. My whole being had been ravaged by the loss of Mia, followed by months of relentless work, and it was now telling me to slow the hell down or face repercussions.

After a whale-watching trip off Sydney Harbour, Stewart and I headed to Cairns with no clue about where to stay, so I asked on Facebook for suggestions, forgetting that most of my traveller followers were young backpackers! However, the first place we stayed in on their advice was really comfortable. We had our own double room overlooking a pool, and although it was spartan, it was clean. Unfortunately, the room was only available for one night. The next hostel we had been advised to check out was a proper backpackers' place, and consequently it had no air conditioning, and cleanliness appeared to be a concept that had eluded the owner. Waking up scratching furiously at huge red blotches from unknown sources, we decided to head on to the next stage of our trip. I could see the attraction to backpackers on tight budgets, though, and I'd stayed in a lot worse as a travel writer for Rough Guides – but at our age we were way past being able to cope without a few of life's small luxuries.

During our brief stay there, we learnt of a young woman whose story reminded me of Tom Webb's. She had fallen from the back of a tractor while working in the Cairns region. When the farmer had seen her injuries, which included a broken collar bone and lacerations, he told her she had to lie to the hospital staff by saying she had fallen while at the hostel rather than at work, or he wouldn't sign off her days. I wondered whether these farms didn't have relevant insurance, or just didn't want their premiums to be affected by a claim. Whichever, it would mean that backpackers missed out on healthcare entitlements if they agreed to these conditions.

The manager of our Cairns hostel appeared fascinated by our story and promised to give me a watch-out list of workplaces and hostels to avoid, which was circulated among backpackers online. Victorian campaigner Robyn Horvath, Andrew Bretherton – an Australian whose girlfriend was carrying out her 88 days under difficult circumstances in North Queensland – and I have since augmented that list considerably through the first-hand accounts we have received from backpackers about their working conditions.

Stewart and I sought sanctuary in the Daintree Rainforest next, and I did my research this time. We stayed in a stunning Queenslander home, with balconies extending around three sides, views across the rainforest and the sound of cassowary calls echoing across the lawns in the morning. In this remote spot it was pretty much impossible to get a phone signal, and we had a couple of days in this beautiful peaceful environment, enjoying the warm rain which drenched us to the skin. We didn't actually see a cassowary but we were entranced by the flocks of fruit bats that descended at dusk, and we managed to startle a bandicoot in our headlights one evening. It was a magical stay, made more sublime by the feeling of having escaped from the hurly-burly of the post–*Australian Story* madness!

One of the important aspects of this trip, which Stewart and I had planned in advance, was the scattering of a vial of Mia's ashes.

This was part of a bigger picture that had been conceived during Mia's cremation in Australia. Having worked with young people in the UK I knew the importance of ritual, especially after calamity. I had witnessed the response to a mining accident when a number of members of a small community in which I was working died down a mine shaft in Meden Vale, Nottinghamshire. The school-children I was teaching wanted to write poems, make pictures and talk about the deaths in a kind of communal grieving, which I thought was their way of making sense of what had happened. I encouraged this, although other teachers complained that the kids were playing on the situation to get out of curriculum work.

Mia's friends also embraced the opportunity to 'celebrate the life', as I encouraged them to do through creativity in redesign-ing the ritual around place and circumstances. We made up small vials of Mia's ashes and put them into pretty blue and orange vel-vet bags, which could be slipped into a purse or vanity case. Her friends could then make little boxes and perch them on mountain tops to photograph, or film scatterings across water, or launch little boats near sacred temples, or scatter the ashes across a bay which they had visited with Mia. The only stipulation I made was that the ashes that went to the Antarctic should be wrapped up, as Mia didn't like the cold. The friend in question went one step further and had a little pouch knitted for the vial.

The plan was for Mia's ashes to continue to travel the world, to places she had loved when she was alive and to places she never managed to visit. We gave out the vials of her ashes both at her memorial on the Gold Coast and at the one in Derbyshire, and they were in high demand. Mia's friends on the Gold Coast were the first to make a video of a scattering, which took place in Byron Bay and set the bar high with a fabulous film of the entire excursion, set to one of Mia's favourite tunes. More followed thick and fast, all shared in a secret social media group. Mia visited Japan, New Zealand, India, Canada . . . the list included more than 50 countries. It was a way for her friends to express both their love for Mia and their grief at losing her, but in a joyous and positive way. Each scattering was different and also creative, and every time footage of a new one arrived I was reduced to both laughter and tears, knowing how much Mia would have appreciated these tributes. They said so much about how well she was loved.

Stewart and I took a boat trip from Cairns out to Fitzroy Island, where we snorkelled with a multitude of fish, a baby shark and even a giant turtle. Stewart scattered Mia's ashes underwater and I made a little film of it. It was jokey and fun, not a serious attempt but something to create a feeling that Mia was there with us, and that she would be there, swimming with the turtles, after we left.

As soon as we got a phone signal on our return to Cairns, Jennifer contacted us asking me to do one last interview, and this one I couldn't resist. One of the most popular radio shows in Australia is Triple J's *Hack*, which is widely listened to by young people, and I was asked to do an interview with them. The interviewer was the first who really challenged me, asking whether I was aware of how prevalent sexual assault was, and that harassment took place in all workplaces.

I replied that most victims would have recourse to the law through the facilities of the police or the Fair Work Ombudsman, and that I would expect the matter to end up resolved either through mediation or in an industrial tribunal. Backpackers' complaints are generally dismissed with: 'It's your word against his, and he's a fine upstanding member of our community, so run along.'

I also pointed out that this was a federal government scheme, and although the backpackers chose to be a part of the 88 days program, there was a degree of compulsion in the linking of the 88 days to the second-year visa. It seemed to me that while the occasional abusive employer might slip through the net, on the whole workers could expect the employers on a government scheme to be vetted in some way for criminal records or any previous complaints of harassment. Instead, there was no vetting, no checks of any kind, and the government could almost be accused of connivance with the criminals and abusers who were taking advantage of young migrant workers by refusing to regulate the system. Surely, I asked, in Australia as with other developed countries, if complaints of sexual harassment are made against state employees – for example public servants, MPs or teachers – the response should be that they're immediately suspended?

On our way to Brisbane we were stopped in the airport in Cairns by someone who recognised me from the ABC documentary. He shook my hand warmly and expressed his admiration for the campaign. He told me he was going to a memorial event for a young woman who had disappeared in the outback and never been found. The meaningless, momentous and life-shattering loss of two young women caused an immediate and unforgettable bond between us. He described how her mother couldn't find a way of coping with her grief, because there had been no body, and therefore no resolution. I felt a cold shiver pass through me as this man described the woman's plight. There but for the grace of God, I thought. The story gave me a strange feeling of thankfulness that there was no doubt left about the who, what and how of Mia's death. The pain of uncertainty must be intolerable. Later, Stewart told me tearfully how impressed he was that I gave time to hear a complete stranger's story, even when we were trying to make a flight. He said I was like Mia in that way, and I suppose that's very true.

Jesse and I were delighted to meet up again. She was incredibly welcoming. We spent a lazy few days together, reminiscing about Mia and enjoying the beaches. Rylea and his cousin took us out on the ocean on jet skis, which was thrilling, but I couldn't help but wish it was Mia there instead of me, as she would have loved it. The other truly amazing experience was to watch feeding time for the pelicans, when the local fish and chip shops go out onto the beach with their waste. Pelicans seem to queue up to be served, then run away from the mob with fish bits sticking from the sides of their beaks! Stewart and I kept looking at each other in astonishment, as we couldn't believe we were watching this on a public beach and not in a zoo. It was one of the funniest sights we witnessed during our entire trip.

A couple of older guys spotted Stewart, Rylea, Jesse and me on the beach and I was surprised when one of them called me away from the scene, to the park bench on which they were seated. I knew he recognised me, and was expecting a good telling off as I surmised from their clothes and walking sticks that they could be members of the farming community. But what he said was, 'You've got some balls, you have, to make that journey across Australia. Good on ya, girl!'

Meanwhile Jennifer fielded the press and found other interviewees, particularly Jennifer Stanger, co-founder of Anti-Slavery Australia in the Faculty of Law at the University of Technology

Sydney, and Alison Rahill of the Freedom Partnership, to speak
to the media, while ABC staff responded to messages that were
coming in thick and fast. I turned on the news one day to hear
Senator Linda Reynolds speaking on behalf of backpackers. I was
in no doubt that she had read all the information I'd sent her after
my second visit to Australia. She spoke so well, using the term
modern slavery to describe the conditions that some of them were
working in. I had carefully avoided this term at all costs because
I know it creates an extreme reaction, so I was pleased that someone in such a position of power had taken up the gauntlet.

After the downtime at the beach, Stewart headed home and
I went on to meet Alison Rahill in Melbourne. I was receiving
more and more messages via email and social media. A young
English woman, Jo-Anne, got in touch to recount her experiences
at a hostel recommended by the federal government's Harvest
Trail initiative. It was originally intended to connect backpackers to legitimate hostels and employers, but like many government
agencies connected to the 88 days scheme it is understaffed and
so under-resourced it has no way of effectively carrying out its
intended function. Jo-Anne talked about herself and other women
feeling uncomfortable after being touched by the hostel owner,
and recounted how he would come into the showers while they
were naked and have full conversations through a glass door, looking directly at them. She described the filth, the stinking sheets,
the decrepit facilities, the lack of security for the inhabitants and
their belongings, strangers entering the premises and the high
rates charged because it was the only backpacker accommodation
in the area.

'We did get work, but never enough to pay rent and eat so we
always owed him.' She said the owner would make them work

around the hostel, undertaking tasks like cleaning, in exchange for accommodation, but at a reduced rate of pay, and with no notice whatsoever. She talked about the boys being employed to dig out asbestos, which was then left close to their living quarters. 'As soon as we mentioned getting the council involved, he concreted it in.' Eventually the backpackers were told to leave with no notice because they had drawn his attention to all the ways he had behaved inappropriately and illegally.

The press was looking for people to continue the conversation post–*Australian Story*, so I asked Jo-Anne if she would speak to a journalist, which she readily agreed to. This added to the mountain of online coverage already given to backpacker stories that week. A few messages came directly through the ABC contact page, for instance a shocking account of mental and verbal abuse in a tiny Queensland township, resulting in a backpacker fleeing after only two weeks, uncertain whether she could stay in Australia a second year, but eager to tell her story once safely back with her partner in Melbourne. It ended, 'The psychological and financial damage it has caused is terrible. Please get back to me about what we can do. Thanks for your time.'

Another message came from someone who had worked as a banana humper, a position reserved for stronger, taller men, which was generally well-paid, but he described how others were treated by the working hostels. People were sacked from the easier jobs on farms on a daily basis, and told to leave the hostels, but without their deposits, which were often retained for spurious reasons.

They charge them for rent knowing no work is coming, then they have to move on after paying up to a month of rent. My best friend's girlfriend booked them onto a farm in the

Northern Territory and the farmer thought two girls were showing up. When he found out my male friend was there he turned very weird. The guy took loads of drugs and alcohol and became abusive and threatening. The day after, two girls showed up and he sacked my friend and his girlfriend before they even did a day's work. They had travelled from Byron Bay just to get there.

A hostel I worked from in Queensland, told a girl she could work for her days. She did three months and asked for her days to be signed as she only had three days on her visa left, and the hostel owner laughed and said, "I can't sign your days off." Three months work and the girl had to go home to Germany. The rules are it's called 88 days. The farmers are telling backpackers it's 88 working days and blagging up to six or seven months out of them. We get a one-year visa and people spend over six months doing farm work.

I also heard from a hostel owner who told me how he had contacted politicians, the media and the Fair Work Ombudsman to try to shine a light on the iniquities of the system. In what was by now a familiar story, she described passports and bonds being retained and backpackers being verbally abused, and kept for much longer than the 88 days, being sent from one employer to another and given a few days' work a week to eke out their time and therefore the money they needed to pay to the hostel. What followed, however, was more concerning:

Some backpackers have been threatened with being hosed down with the fire hose and threatened with having drugs planted on them, and the police rung. The owners will not lock external doors and one girl woke up one night to find a strange man masturbating over her bed.

The owners of another hostel came to our hostel and threatened a girl with breaking her legs because she left their place. The police will not do anything as backpackers are only here for a short time, and the backpackers don't want to be caught up in an ongoing court drama.

These were just some of a stack of messages which had been pouring in to the ABC from viewers and those who had picked up on the story through social media. I realised I had my work cut out for me on my return to the UK.

I was doing well with getting attention from the press, but the politicians still seemed loath to meet me. Alison and I did manage to make contact with Professor Allan Fels of the Migrant Workers' Taskforce. The meeting was odd. Fels turned up wearing what looked like his gardening gear (he obviously didn't count the meeting as a photo opportunity then!) and instead of listening to what I had to say, he told us about his own work exposing the 7-Eleven wage fraud scandal, and then went on to explain how fractious the working party had already become, with so many disparate interests involved. I suspected he didn't want to add yet another example of exploitation into the mix, but I felt frustrated as this was the most likely home for a governmental investigation into the 88 days sceme. It was probably for this reason that, even though the taskforce was meeting while I was in Melbourne, Fels point blank refused to let me join it. Many of my allies were attending and thought I should be there, and I was even in the building while they all filed past: my NUW compatriots, Dr Elsa Underhill of Deakin University, co-author of the report on temporary workers' safety whose house I was staying at while I was in Melbourne, Tom O'Shea of Fair Work who'd met with me on a previous visit. I suspect they thought I would gatecrash anyway, but I decided to maintain a dignified stance, as I thought my absence would speak louder than my presence, and in any case, union reps made a point at the outset of flagging that they thought I should be there.

The process of making a documentary is certainly not for the faint-hearted. Filming takes over your life for the duration, and everything is seen through the prism of a camera lens, whether it's social events, political liaisons or personal downtime. It had been intrusive in the extreme, because that's exactly what the process requires. If I had been working with another set of people, I think it would have been intolerable. But with Jennifer Feller at the helm and with Alison Rahill as a comrade-in-arms, and the likes of Stewart, Jenny Stanger, Elsa Underhill, Matt Pulford, Jayne, Jesse, Daniel and Chris in the wings to offer either professional and informational input or a shoulder to cry on, or even just a proper mickey-take and subsequent belly laugh to bring me crashing back down to earth when it was required, it became pleasurable. I was treated with respect by professionals and given the chance to explore my own feelings about campaigning, and about the documentary as a form of communication, but I was in no danger of taking myself too seriously either.

The impact the documentary had on its audience could be measured by the unprecedented level of responses from viewers and the press, as well as from online comments. One reviewer put it succinctly: 'I was beginning to think there was nothing new under the (*Australian Story*) sun, until I saw last night's episode. But the incredible story of that woman journeying across Australia after the terrible loss of her daughter had me gripped from start to finish.'

While I'd been reluctant to carry out all the media work, I have to admit that the piece Rachael produced for BBC Radio Derby was electrifying, so much so that I couldn't even listen to it on a first attempt. I heard later that listeners in the UK were deeply affected by it. While sensational, documentaries can change hearts and minds, and I think we managed to get more people on board through that radio piece in the UK and through the two TV episodes of *Australian Story* in Australia.

But I had no idea where to go from there. I decided to be guided by fate. If the press interest faded, I would call it a day for the time being, and go back to the peace and quiet of the Derbyshire hills. I was certainly ready for a break. I had been advised by Paul Broadbent right at the beginning of the campaign trail that it would take a lifetime to achieve change in this field, so I felt I needed to pace myself or I was going to burn out too soon, and although I wasn't prepared to stop campaigning until the last avenue was explored, I had no idea if I would ever see any concrete changes.

15

Surviving the Grief

On my return to the UK at the end of July 2017, I was in a strange, dislocated place. It was less than a year after Mia's death. I was no longer teaching as I hadn't felt able to return to work. The idea of facing a classroom of students in my still fragile state was horrifying, not because of the capacity of young people to be cruel – which I was aware of, but could have received with equanimity – but because I knew they had a similar capacity for empathy and I didn't want them placing themselves in my shoes. I had returned to work the day after my father's death (even though the school provided cover for me) and I realised I'd returned too soon when I found myself welling up with grief as I recited one of Simon Armitage's poems about his relationship with his father. I left the room briefly and came back to see one of my Year 11s in floods of tears, who explained later she couldn't bear to see me in pain! How could I inflict this level of emotion on young people? Selfishly, at that point I also wasn't sure how I could cope with the envy I would feel as other people's children learnt and flourished when mine was dead in the ground.

More positively, our renovations had gone well and the house was now a home, decorated to my and Stewart's tastes. The project had gone as far as it could without an injection of cash from my recent inheritance, which I was unwilling to commit. The proposed extension had been intended both as business premises for Mia to use as a preschool nursery, and as a way of adding value to the house for the future, which Mia, and Stewart's two daughters – Charlotte and Emily – would inherit. This incentive was now diminished, and I no longer felt committed to my life in Cromford or to life at all, in fact. I fended off thoughts of suicide and fought against feelings of depression.

At one point I acquired mild antidepressants from the doctor. I took one, then mused about whether my mood had lifted, knowing full well it doesn't happen that quickly. I realised that if the tablet lifted my mood I would feel conflicted, for being incapable of controlling my own moods and in need of pharmaceuticals would paradoxically produce a sense of failure. Luckily, I had Stewart by my side, and he understood all of this because of similar thoughts around his brother's suicide. Like me, he finds solace in hard work and its results, and so everything I did to memorialise Mia's life was with his blessing. I threw the rest of the antidepressants in the bin and decided to carry on campaigning instead.

The website www.88daysandcounting.com was almost ready to become a one-stop shop for information on the 88 days program. Most of all I wanted to provide a platform for reviews of all kinds of businesses used by young people embarking on the program, including farms, hostels and employment agencies. Sheffield-based Mantra Media had completed the framework while I was in Australia, and the site now awaited the huge number of responses we'd received from a survey I had circulated on various backpacker sites.

Inputting the information was a slow and laborious task, and I recruited some willing helpers, including Kay, Tom Jackson's girlfriend, who did some sterling work in Tom's memory. The majority of the work, however, was down to me. Happily, it kept me occupied, and it felt as if I was doing something of benefit.

On 25 May 2017, even before the documentary had aired, we had woken to fantastic news from Australia. It looked as if the campaign for better working conditions was finally having an impact: a Labour Hire Licensing Bill had been submitted to the Queensland parliament for proposed implementation in August 2018. This was an important initial step in creating a system of control for contractors and working hostels with regard to how they treat backpackers. On the passing of the bill into law, Grace Grace, the minister for employment and industrial relations, introduced the scheme, and in her straight-talking manner listed a number of the abuses we had discovered while campaigning:

> Shonks, shysters and cheats have brought Queensland's labour hire industry into disrepute. For far too long, dodgy operators have been blatantly exploiting vulnerable workers and ripping off those without the power to fight back. Just last week an investigation was launched into a labour hire operator in the Lockyer Valley for alleged underpayment of wages, the provision of unsafe accommodation and unsafe drinking water

and unregistered transport. To make matters worse, it's even alleged some of the workers were charged job finding fees – it doesn't get much lower than that.

The new scheme meant that employers would have to: pass a fit-and-proper person test; comply with workplace laws, including workplace compensation, wages and superannuation; pay a licence; and report regularly on their operations.

Over the following months, the states of South Australia and Victoria followed suit – South Australia introducing their bill on 10 August 2017 and Victoria introducing theirs in December 2017. The Victorian legislation was probably the most considered, as it was informed by Professor Anthony Forsyth's comprehensive report. In addition to Queensland's measures, Victoria included the establishment of a public register of labour hire providers, and a Labour Hire Licensing Authority whose remit is to monitor and investigate compliance. Operators that do not hold a licence, or breach the conditions of it, are liable for both civil and criminal penalties. All three state legislatures were in accord, however, that the legislation needed to be implemented on a federal level, otherwise criminals would use loopholes by operating across state borders.

Earlier in the year I had started a Facebook group specifically around the 88 days. This was far more immediate than the website we were building since it could react to information as it emerged, and provide a forum for backpackers to ask questions and be given immediate feedback regarding prospective employers. It was not only proving a popular place to flag general safety issues but also as a means of avoiding unscrupulous operators. I had become an unofficial conduit for information from the Department of Immigration and Border Protection to backpackers, and from backpackers to the National Crime Agency. This was never a role I'd intended to adopt, but the staff who manned the immigration information phone hotline were notoriously ill-informed regarding issues to do with the 88 days scheme, and at the time the Fair Work Ombudsman would only escalate around fifty cases a year to the courts. As far as casual labourers were concerned, there was little point contacting the Fair Work Ombudsman since as a casual worker you could be dismissed the following day by your employer should a complaint be made to the authorities.

One of the people who contacted me through the Facebook page was a twenty-five-year-old who wrote to me from a 15,000-acre cattle ranch and was in the throes of a difficult situation. 'The position required me to cut posts for a 15 km fence, welding, horse riding and taking care of the horses, two pups and the dogs,' she began. The dogs numbered twenty in total. She talked about the isolation, the need for a generator and the lack of any phone signal, an issue that compounds problems for isolated backpackers on the 88 days. Sometimes the farmer was verbally abusive towards her 'for no reason. And sexual comments. After these few occasions I talked about his behaviour with my colleague and we agreed that it was not okay.' She explained a series of incidents, where her employer's temper was gradually rising because a felled tree landed the wrong way, followed by a dog fight where he thumped one of the dogs in the face. At this point she intervened on behalf of the dog.

> He just said, 'Shut up, you fucking cunt and get the fuck in the car.' He said he [the dog] was worth shooting, it was a softy and that would mean the other dogs had nothing to fight about anymore. After this I lost count of the verbal abuse

towards me; I just had enough and decided I wanted to leave, but I had to think this through . . .

With tears in my eyes we drove home, where I went straight to my room, cried a little bit and decided I wanted to have a conversation with my employer about what just happened, that I do not accept that and I want to look for a different job. I made it clear I respect him as a farmer, but talking to me like that numerous times and treating animals the way he does, I didn't accept that. I said I would like my paperwork and money as soon as possible. He promised me this for over a few weeks but nothing happened. He was mad again, telling me I was useless, then in the same sentence he would say he wouldn't want me to leave, then was mad again and wouldn't get the paperwork sorted for me. In the end he 'promised' to get the paperwork the next day [Tuesday] and be back late in the afternoon, and I 'can fuck off after'. He said I'm 'just like all the city bastards and I belong on the beach'.

The young woman took his car the next morning without asking and drove into town to the local police station.

He's obviously known by the local police. Questions were: 'Is he talking to himself?' 'No.' 'Has he got weapons?' 'Yes.' 'Has he threatened to use them?' 'Yes. He said he didn't like the government or law enforcement in any way and he will shoot.' Anyway, that was enough information to accompany me back to the farm to get my stuff. So I took my stuff with one officer looking out to see if he was coming and the other one making sure I was okay. Even the officer said, 'Let's get out of here before he comes back.' That's when I noticed police had extra guns in the back of the car and there were bulletproof vests lying beside me.

She then described how the police took her to the relative safety of a local caravan park where she stayed for two nights in recovery, then headed to a larger town. What she wanted, however, was pay for the five weeks she'd worked, and paperwork towards her 88 days, which needed signing off.

I did my best for this young woman. I started by contacting Alison Rahill, who was at a wedding in Thailand at the time, so she put me in touch with a Salvation Army colleague who she assured me would be a sympathetic and helpful contact, as she was from a social work background. However, the first thing this colleague told me was that Australian farmers might be a bit sweary, but they were generally good people. I persevered, reiterating how frightened he'd made her, and how the police had been wary of him themselves. She said she'd do some research and come back to me. Her follow-up email said that she'd found out through local knowledge that the farmer in question was mentally unstable, and therefore I couldn't expect her, or anyone else locally, to go with the backpacker to ask for her paperwork to be signed!

While I appreciated her reticence, the situation remained unresolved. A man who locals – even a social worker – were too afraid to approach was still perfectly eligible to take part in the 88 days scheme, and there was nothing I could do about it.

Although backpackers continued to contact me, and press like *Grazia UK* and *Marie Claire Australia* were also getting in touch for interviews, this was altogether a quieter time as I'd anticipated.

I found the constant flow of adrenaline required for coping, first with Mia's death and then the manic few weeks of filming the documentary, had left me vulnerable to experiencing adrenal rushes. I experienced them if I caught anything violent on TV, and almost every morning on waking.

My coping mechanisms concentrated on exercise, especially long dog walks in our beautiful Derbyshire countryside. I continued my daily yoga routine with meditation sessions and managed my diet carefully.

There were days when missing Mia was so painful I didn't want to get out of bed, especially during the winter months, which are dreadfully cold in our hilly county. As time went on, I felt her presence less and less and I was desperate to remember and to immortalise her.

A friend who had been on a shamanistic training course told me she was asked to try to establish contact with someone who had died suddenly. She said she immediately thought of Mia, and made a shamanistic journey to find Mia in the place between life and death. My friend asked Mia if she was happy in that place. Mia had replied that, yes, she wanted to be there, because she needed to be near to me and make sure I was alright. This was a lovely thing to tell me, although it had taken her a while to do so. As soon as she said it, though, I thought back and realised I was communing with Mia much less frequently, and that if she had been watching over me she no longer was. I felt bereft all over again, and I shed bitter tears at the thought that Mia might believe I had moved on and stopped grieving her. But I was also glad that Mia might think I was strong enough for her to let go.

And I was strong enough, for sure. If I ever asked myself the question 'Why me?', I already knew the answer: 'Because you're strong enough. You won't go under.'

At home I surveyed the jungle of a garden that had first attracted us to our house. It looked immense. Rather than take it on in one go, I decided to memorialise Mia by creating a tiny garden in a wooden pallet (of the kind used for transporting goods on trucks). Our local show, Celebrating Cromford, had an annual tradition of locals and businesses creating pallet gardens, so I decided to concentrate on a display of blue and gold flowers and place it outside our house in the street. When I first arrived in Australia, one of the things Jesse was doing for the memorial we held on the Gold Coast was buying blue and gold balloons to be released. I was a little perplexed because I know what havoc they can wreak on the environment, but the purchase had been made and I'd already upset the girls once by sharing my misgivings about their social media profiles, so I held my tongue! (As I'd done when I'd seen Mia releasing paper lanterns at the Loi Krathong festival of light on the Thailand leg of her travels.)

I was interested by the choice of colours, so I asked Jesse why she'd chosen them, and she said they were Mia's favourites. This made me laugh, as not long before she'd left for Australia Mia and I had had a conversation about favourite colours, and I'd told her that blue and gold were mine because they reminded me of the sea and the sand. Mia had reacted with derision! Similarly, shortly after the first anniversary of Mia's death, Elliot had come round for a visit. He'd bought me a gift of some wind chimes, and we sat going through photos and talking about Mia. I mentioned the choice of colours for the balloons, and Elliot too expressed his surprise. 'It's just, I once bought her some orange roses and she told me off, because she said she didn't like the colour orange!'

As he was leaving, I offered Elliot a keepsake and he asked whether he could have a favourite book of Mia's, about the artist

Banksy. I said of course he should take it, and as he opened it to flick through the pages he found the orange roses, pressed between the pages! We were both subjected to a fresh wave of emotion by the coincidence, and we each tried not to show the other the tears we were fighting. It really felt to me like the sweetest apology from Mia for her somewhat callous disregard for Elliot's gift!

So the memorial pallet garden was a basic gold and blue colour scheme, with sunflowers, scabiosa, campanula, geum, daisies and ferns. The words 'Fly High Mia' were incorporated in eight-centimetre-high wooden letters, with a gold and blue paper kite pinned to the tree behind. I also added in rosemary for remembrance – and honesty, to reflect Mia's integrity. As it turned out I had far too many plants for the pallet, so I ended up digging a whole bed. Gradually this has grown to incorporate more and more of the garden, as Stewart provides me with the infrastructure of terraces and raised beds, as well as a pond with a little waterfall, water butts and a corner for composting. When our dear lurcher, Nancy, died, she was buried along with a vial of Mia's ashes next to the pond, and I bought a stone statue of a seated lurcher in her memory. I now grow nearly everything from seed and include fruit trees and beds of vegetables for our own consumption.

Mia's friends also fundraised for a bench, which we commissioned from local artist David Turner. He created a thing of wonder out of galvanised wrought iron, featuring a wilderness of wrought iron plants and, again, the kite motif. The bench is situated on a nearby hilltop overlooking a valley and the farm belonging to our dear friends Ned and Joe, where Mia worked and looked after their three kids, and learnt to value nature, children and her skills as a carer. Around the bench, as well as building a stalwart fence to keep the cows away from the metalwork, the Wiltshire family have planted trees in Mia's memory, including Rowan's namesake tree which takes pride of place. The views are panoramic and breathtaking, especially at sunset in summer and autumn when Mia's presence can be felt in the intense colours of the sky, in wisps of cloud and in the flurries of wind that lift the branches and whisper through the leaves. This has become my go-to place when I need to be alone with my tears, my memories and my grief.

16

Campaigning On – A Modern Slavery Act

SINCE MY VISIT TO THE UK HIGH COMMISSION DURING THE FILM-ing of *Australian Story*, Menna Rawlings had acted fast, establishing a hotline for backpackers on their web page, a forum of regular meetings for representatives from the relevant consulates to exchange information on backpacker issues, and a contact for me to send information to directly. At last I had somewhere to go with some of the backpackers' most pressing concerns: the UK's National Crime Agency team in Australia were working with the Australian Federal Police, Australian Border Force and state police forces. Kasandra and Mark at the Foreign and Commonwealth Office were well placed to intervene on British backpackers' behalf. For backpackers of other nationalities, Kasandra had to go to the respective consulates, which was not ideal, but as an interim step it was better than nothing. When I explained my frustration about backpackers not feeling they could report to Australian authorities, Kasandra replied by email:

A lack of reporting to local authorities does not necessarily mean we cannot take action through the Australian system as it is not only the policing stream that deal with these matters. For example, the agency responsible for compliance of employers and who approve/revoke their status in the 417 Visa system are separate to the police as is the agency responsible for granting/refusing 417 extension applications. These are some of the levers we have available to gather evidence for prosecution of employers, individuals, etc.

Our approach is understandably multi-faceted and may appear complex from the outside, but from within, we are working in unison with these agencies which will yield the best result from a prosecution angle.

The more of these employers/individuals that we can have shut down and bring charges against, the stronger the message we can deliver within the 417 visa system that these actions will not be tolerated and will be closely monitored and breaches prosecuted.

A safer environment for those visiting Australia, from not only the UK, is the end game for not only the NCA, HMG and the FCO, but also the Australian agencies that we are working with.

Kasandra made it clear in other emails that between us we were making an impact, but knowing I was campaigning she urged me not to share the information she divulged as it could have interfered with current police operations.

A referral mailbox the NCA set up for backpackers to report their experiences pulled in 400 emails in the first six weeks. In working with state and federal agencies such as the Australian Tax

Office and Fair Work Ombudsman, NCA in Australia has since achieved some notable successes, resulting in the prosecution and conviction of a rapist and others taking advantage of young back-packers trying to complete their 88 days.

A Modern Slavery Act was long overdue in Australia – slavery was yet to be abolished. Paul Broadbent of GLAA had made me aware that an act was on the agenda when I started campaigning. My concern was that the 88 days program and the potential for exploitation of young people on it should be recognised as part of the anti-slavery agenda.

Just before what would have been Mia's twenty-second birth-day, in October 2017, I was contacted by Alison Rahill asking me if I wanted to make a trip out to Mildura in Victoria to address the only regional hearing of the inquiry into establish-ing a Modern Slavery Act in Australia. This was aptly situated, as the Sunraysia district was notorious for stories of ill-treatment of migrant workers of all nationalities, both documented and undocumented.

Alison pointed out that this was the only way we were going to get the issues documented on Hansard (the report of the proceed-ings of the parliament and its committees), which was important from a campaigning point of view – particularly, for me, to high-light the iniquities of the 88 days program, and to establish the connection between the 88 days and the anti-slavery agenda. It was an opportunity not to be missed.

There was an additional pull too. Before I had left Australia on my last visit, Sally McManus of the Australian Council of Trade Unions had promised to ask the then leader of the opposition Bill Shorten to meet me. I had heard he'd agreed to this readily. So I planned a trip at the last minute, incorporating both of these meetings, with time to catch up with a few friends and allies on the way.

I was nervous about going to Mildura as I really didn't know what to expect, and my fears were only exacerbated by a conversation with a member of staff from the Freedom Partnership just before I left London. Heather Moore, who would be travelling with me when I reached Australia, informed me that a local MP for Townsville, Queensland, had chastised her because of the Freedom Partnership's involvement with me. Heather also relayed that one of the notorious farmers was complaining about our website, because she felt she'd been treated unjustly by us. The farmer in question had complained to Queensland's horticulture industry body – Growcom – who had in turn said they would refuse to work with the Freedom Partnership unless they cut ties with me. All this was delivered to me minutes before I was about to get on my flight from London.

Needless to say, I didn't sleep on that journey and I was incredibly anxious by the time I reached Sydney. To make matters worse, Alison Rahill wasn't in Sydney, she was out in the regions preparing Pacific Islanders to speak at the Mildura public hearing. The hotel I had booked was quite a miserable affair, and I was feeling sorry for myself and entirely deflated by the time I arrived in Canberra.

Canberra may be renowned for being boring, but it is beautiful – second only to Sydney in its choice of majestic situation. As I approached the city, its valley location among softly rolling hills took my breath away, but I had very little time for sightseeing. By the time I met Heather I'd spoken to Alison, who explained that I didn't need to be too concerned about the position taken by Growcom as she'd calmed the troubled waters in her famously diplomatic manner. I wasn't surprised as she'd kept me calm throughout the whole filming process, and I was well aware of her diplomatic skills.

My first port of call was the UK High Commission, where I caught up with Menna Rawlings. She was conducting a wedding for a gay couple that day – a service provided for UK citizens by the High Commission prior to the legalisation of equal marriage in Australia – so our meeting was brief. However, invaluably, I met my contact Kasandra Perry for the first time.

The name Kasandra Perry conjured for me a veneer of slick sophistication and placatory soundbites, and I was astonished when Kasandra herself appeared. I felt a sense of kinship immediately as, far from the slightly distant office type I'd conjured up in my imagination, she was completely solid and down-to-earth, emanating goodwill, humour, competence and reliability, and above all a sense of compassion. As she relayed stories of some of her escapades during her years at the Foreign and Commonwealth Office and National Care Agency I realised she was highly experienced and well regarded, and she laughed at my expression of delight at her evident seniority and track record. 'They didn't just employ me for my looks, you know!' she growled with a wry grin.

Despite her experience, Kasandra admitted that the sheer volume of stories I had presented her with to date had reduced her to tears at one point, and she'd actually been offered compassionate leave by her manager. Her sense of outrage was palpable. As she put it, 'This was not the Australia I grew up in.'

She also took pains to explain to me how much of a difference the campaign was making. She couldn't give very much away, but she reassured me that all kinds of things were happening behind the scenes, from police raids in the areas renowned for

backpacker abuse, to additional police training, and the discip-
lining of under-performing officers in the regions. In fact, some were
being moved from one station to another where it was considered
their local affiliations were impeding justice to operations.

I was pleased to hear from a professional that my hard work
since Mia's death was already having an impact on the circumstances of so many other backpackers up and down the country.
But knowing the scale of the task still ahead of us, I couldn't help
but wonder whether sufficient resources were being deployed.
Nevertheless, it was clear there was a will to change among
civil servants.

From the High Commission, Heather and I headed straight
to parliament. This was a historic day as Bill Shorten's former
union offices had just been raided by the police on allegations
of corruption – we felt incredibly honoured that the leader of
the opposition still managed to keep the appointment with us.
In fact, not only did he meet us, but he pledged to form a Labor
Party working group to deal with the issues. One of the ways in
which worker rights could be protected in Australia was through
union involvement, and I had been discussing how best this could
be achieved since the early days of the campaign, particularly
with members of the National Union of Workers. What I wanted
most of all was a concessionary fee for backpackers, because their
wages were often too negligible for them to afford union fees.
I brought up the subject with Shorten and he agreed with me.
I knew that the stumbling block would be getting the idea past
union officials, understanding that some members would be sup-
porting entire families on award wages, and would not appreciate

that piece rates could leave backpackers out of pocket even after they had been paid.

It was at parliament where I managed to catch up with Linda Reynolds, a senator for Western Australia, and thank her for a press interview in which she'd been so supportive of the campaign.

From Canberra I drove the 800 kilometres to Mildura alone, and still my anxieties were high. I'd agreed to meet a hostel owner who calls himself Bobby Moore online. He wanted to show me around the area, and I had no idea whether he was friend or foe – I didn't even know his real name. I had intended to find a motel and sleep on the way, but as it transpired I drove straight past my intended stopover, so I just carried on driving. I was astonished to see mobs of emu, and I anxiously scanned the road for errant kangaroos, in terror after hearing stories of what they could do to a car, but more to the point what a car could do to them.

I arrived in Mildura in the early hours of the morning and since it was too early to get breakfast I headed out of town and found a path leading alongside the majestic Murray River.

I sat on the bank, admiring the steady pace of the immense, sparkling sunlit river, the red gums that bordered the tranquil path and the insistent morning call of a kookaburra in the trees. Reminiscent of the Mississippi, I could quite imagine Tom Sawyer and Huck Finn appearing at any moment around a bend on an ancient paddle steamer. The place seemed absolutely delightful, and I struggled to equate this almost mystical scene with some of the horror stories I'd heard.

I later learnt of an ugly story connected to a paddle steamer which had been used as accommodation for backpackers, and apparently ended in the death of a young man who had dived drunkenly from its deck before it was condemned as unsafe for habitation. Even the beautiful, fast-moving Murray seemed somehow to conspire against backpackers in this seemingly lovely little town.

Feeling anxious and exhausted, at the appointed time I went to meet Bobby Moore in a fast-food vendor's carpark. There were two guys in the car, and as I got in I wondered how stupid I was being, and how often I warned backpackers not to do this very thing without alerting a friend, taking a photograph of the licence plate, and agreeing a time to check in with a friend afterwards. Nobody knew I was even in Mildura yet!

Fortunately I needn't have worried. The men were John George, aka Bobby Moore, and his son Craig, both of whom I'd spoken to at length online. While Craig was visibly irritated by everything I said in defence of backpackers, and pretty soon stormed out of the car in disgust, his father was affable enough, even quite charming, and he took me on a long tour of hostels, campsites and local landmarks, explaining the workings of local industries, which was mainly grape and citrus production, both for table and wineries. He also informed me that the hostels had just been inspected by the council, which I thought was interesting timing given the arrival of the regional hearing of the inquiry into establishing a Modern Slavery Act in town, but he did let slip that this was the first inspection for nine years.

We visited the town of Red Cliffs and he introduced me to Big Lizzie, an impressively massive 45-tonne traction engine originally used to clear the mallee scrub. The sheer size and magnificence of Lizzie was incredibly evocative of the hardship of the lives of the original settlers, and of their incredible frontiersmanship in settling a harsh, unforgiving land. It was no wonder that there could be such a culture clash between the farmers who had taken on the mantle of these settlers and the backpackers who landed in these places, often straight out of school, with no knowledge of the dangers or hardships that were second nature to outbackers.

I headed on to the accommodation I'd booked through Airbnb. I arrived at the property not really knowing what to expect as there had only been a handful of photos of it online, but I was delighted by the building's grand, Queenslander-style charm, its broad wraparound balcony and its riverside location, complete with landing stage. A cool, ageless interior completed the effect of calm and luxury.

I'd rented this spacious villa because I was expecting company, and the first person to arrive was Robyn Horvath. Robyn had contacted me in the early days of the campaign as she'd helped a number of backpackers over the years down in Morwell, the small industrial town where she lived. Robyn had already given me refuge in her hometown on my first visit to Victoria. She was a delightful and comforting person to be around, really caring and watchful of my state of mind. She had been a single parent of an only child, so she was aware of what I was going through, and she also supported the campaign as she'd seen first-hand how difficult life could be for backpackers completing their 88 days. One of the reports I received through Robyn was the first of many about a hostel in South Australia. The backpacker said that a hostel owner who lived in a caravan on his own site had effectively taken him hostage on a seven-hour trip into the bush while the owner injected himself with ice in front of him. 'The next day I was informed that he had set his bus [his home] on fire after what I can only assume was a paranoid episode on realising I had left – all of his drugs and drug-taking happened on the bus. Animals were killed in the fire and he and [his girlfriend] lost all of their personal belongings.'

The backpacker was still contemplating sharing his story with the media in order to raise awareness and prevent it from happening to anyone else, but was terrified of this man and extremely conflicted after learning about his mental problems.

Irony of ironies, the property I'd rented through Airbnb, this coolly magnificent, porticoed open-plan villa, belonged to one of the big local wineries, who no doubt employed backpackers to pick their grapes. As I surveyed the surroundings somewhat guiltily, I had to wonder whether they paid decent rates or not. The walls displayed photos of three generations of a charmingly handsome family and I found it hard to believe they weren't as kind as their pictures suggested.

Anyway, as 'ladies of a certain age', Robyn and I were comfortable in its faded glory. We feasted on their oranges and the bottle of wine left for us, and really enjoyed the fin-de-siècle charm of the place, not to mention the thought of sleeping on clean, fresh bed linen.

After a couple of hours, two lads I knew through social media arrived from Melbourne, having shared a lift up together. They were Laurent, a Belgian backpacker, and Andrew Bretherton, the Australian whose girlfriend was doing her 88 days. Andrew has given immeasurable support to the campaign and to me personally through his online presence and through liaising with the unions. He works as an administrator on the Facebook Group 88 Days and Counting, and has a measured and constant sense of social justice and a hypervigilance for trolls and abusive posting on the page.

Andrew first contacted me about the situation his girlfriend was in with a company that offers labour hire services and had recently been convicted of exploiting workers. The girlfriend emailed me an account of her exploitation, which was a familiar story of gross underpayment and intimidation. Andrew and I had done what we could to help her, reporting the situation to the Fair Work Obudsman and the AWU union official in the area, while maintaining her anonymity. The result so far was that the company realised who had made the complaints and promoted her, but left her colleagues in the same situation Andrew Bretherton's girlfriend described.

Laurent, on the other hand, had contacted me to tell me about the attempted rape of a male friend of his that he witnessed in a caravan park, and how the owner had rehoused the perpetrator in a hotel in order to remove him from the scene without sacking him. He was part of a group of foreigners who stay at the same site every year, and was a very fast picker, so Laurent suspected this was why the owner wanted to protect him. Laurent and his friends moved to another hostel as they no longer felt safe in the unlock-able caravans. The owner then fired them, depriving them of work unless they stayed at his caravan park.

Having this time together in such a calm and peaceful location was a wonderful opportunity for me, Laurent and Andrew to relax and share stories, and feel the kind of kinship that merely chat-ting online can't provide. We were united in our distress over the 88 days scheme, but also in a strong belief that we needed to grasp the opportunity to tell our stories to this influential audience in the hope of leaving a legacy of change for those who came in our wake. We felt powerful together, as we knew we were covering all bases: first-hand backpacker accounts, combined with the voices of campaigners at home and abroad, not least that of Robyn.

After enjoying glasses of fresh orange juice, which Laurent thoughtfully prepared for us from the oranges in the garden,

the four of us headed into town to meet up with Alison Rahill
and some of the Pacific Islanders. I was also delighted to become
reacquainted with Moe Turaga, the lovely Fijian I had met while
filming *Australian Story*.

Alison had her own stories to tell that afternoon. She had been
to nearby Robinvale to see the charred remains of a burnt-out share
house from which the occupants had narrowly escaped with their
lives. She met undocumented workers who were living in appall-
ing, cramped and unsanitary conditions, earning so little that they
were struggling to feed themselves, let alone send money home
to their families. I had heard so many awful stories, but still I felt
the tears welling as I heard of yet more anguish among migrant
workers. I felt that we were stronger together, and this made me
even more determined to continue with the campaign.

First on the agenda the next day was a meeting organised by the
Salvation Army. This was ostensibly a welcome and a get-together
for everyone who was speaking the following day at the parliamentary hearing. It gave us an opportunity to meet each other
and to listen to each other's stories, all told from the heart without
the constraints of the inquiry's formalities. I was disappointed to
learn that the National Union of Workers had declined to attend
this meeting, as I felt we were all working for the same cause,
but the political aspects of the campaign were frequently going
to be challenging for me to navigate, and were the main reason I
hadn't wanted to form strong political allegiances with one party
or another. I know it's important to have as many strings to your
bow as possible as a campaigner, and this was most certainly a
cross-party issue.

A number of speakers gave moving accounts of their involvement in modern slavery, and what it meant to them and the people they represented. I wasn't the only person who was in tears that day. Then it was time for my speech.

I introduced myself, and then the campaign. I spoke of the vulnerability of migrant workers, especially backpackers. I explained that while some of the backpackers on the 88 days scheme were indeed gap-year students looking to prolong their experience abroad, others were economic migrants.

Just like your forbears, they may have struggled to raise the funds to reach your shores. Instead they travel here with a view to settling in your country, and however unrealistic we know that to be, that is the dream which adds further to their vulnerability. They will do just about anything to achieve that dream, and they have self-selected for tenacity and endurance. Even when they recognise what the 88 days can entail in terms of exploitation, they stick with the program, because it is potentially one of the doorways they need to traverse to attain a better way of life.

I then went on to describe the working conditions many young people were experiencing, and how these were the norm rather than the exception.

So after arriving at their working hostel, they can be asked for a large sum of money up-front – from $500 to even $1000 – which is a bond to be returned when they have given two weeks' notice to leave. (Bear in mind that as casual workers they can be dismissed on the spot.) They have been promised work, and expect to begin on the Monday after they arrive. Their passports may or may not be taken 'for safe keeping'.

The work doesn't materialise. They sit and wait, the weeks pass, and then the work starts to dribble in, but it may be only a couple of mornings a week. They cannot leave, however, as they need to give two weeks' notice. So they wait. They may be aware that the piece rates they are earning are low, and that the promises they receive have been reneged on, so they complain. Others arrive and the hostel is continually kept full of expectant workers, but only a select few are given full days. If they continue to complain, they become 'troublesome', so when their savings are completely gone and their debts start to mount up, the hostel owner says, 'You need to pay me what you owe me, or leave.' At this point the youngsters are supposed to call home, but if they don't have that option they're in trouble.

So someone who has no recourse to extra funds can be put out on the street. But not only that, hostel owners have their own networks and have been known to contact other owners in the neighbourhood to ensure individuals are not taken in anywhere else in the locale. They are labelled as troublemakers.

I want you to consider where they can go in your country at this point, because if you know of anywhere they can turn to, please contact me. As yet I have not found a single place they can go.

I wanted to finish on a high note and be positive about the situation, and I claimed things were improving. But I discovered that evening that my optimism was misplaced. We went to dinner in a big group again, this time with the very approachable MP Chris Crewther, chair of the inquiry into establishing a Modern Slavery Act. I asked him what he wanted from me at the inquiry, and he replied he wanted anecdotes, which was more or less what I had prepared.

As we were eating I managed to reach out to a young back-packer called Rob Clark, who had first contacted me to raise his concerns about a working hostel. Rob was putting in long shifts and wasn't able to attend the formal meeting the following day, but he turned up that evening at the restaurant after most of the assembled company had departed. I found Rob to be an incredibly astute person.

He hadn't been staying in the main hostel but in an annexe, where he said there were no members of the management team or staff on duty during the night, that fire doors were kept locked at all times, that fire alarms were not hard wired and had no batteries, that the place was alive with rats, and that there were insufficient toilets and showers for the numbers sharing the annexe. He took Andrew to the area with him and showed him around the hostel. Andrew took photographs of the flooded toilets and cramped conditions, but said what shocked him the most was the disgusting smell from what had once served as a swimming pool and now appeared to be an open sewer. All of this in a hostel that had passed a council inspection with flying colours the same week! Rob said he had been around at the time of the inspection and felt there was an overly friendly relationship between inspectors and hostel owners. He also said that there were live-in drug dealers in most of the hostels in that area.

*

The following day was the only regional hearing of the inquiry into establishing a Modern Slavery Act, and as such it was a historical and sober occasion. Much of it was formal, procedural and quite drawn out, but some of the accounts we heard were shocking. I was pleased that Laurent and Andrew's accounts were well received.

Also startling and incredibly powerful was the account given by a Malaysian journalist, Saiful Hasam, a reporter with the newspaper *Utusan Malaysia*, who went undercover to expose exploitation in Victoria's fruit-picking industry. The stories he told were familiar, but more startling due to the undocumented status of the workers. Fruit pickers were lured to Australia with promises of high incomes, Hasam said. When they arrived they were paid a pittance, kept in overcrowded homes with exorbitant rent and effectively trapped in debt bondage.

Hasam warned the inquiry that exploitation was occurring on a significant scale. He had arrived in Australia in 2016, posing as a fruit picker who was prepared to work illegally. He was paid $110 for 24 hours work over four days. About $80 went to pay rent in a small home he shared with eleven other workers, mostly from Malaysia. He was short-changed $10 by his contractor, leaving him with just $20.

'The story is basically the same, sad story,' Hasam said. 'A thousand sad stories, they are basically the same story. They are struggling. For the newbies, they are struggling and keep thinking, "Today I have to plant so many trees just to pay rent. After that part, then we are struggling to collect enough money for food."

'Sometimes, based on my experience, it's just enough for food and rent . . . This is grossly unfair for the workers, because they are very hard-working.'

Hasam was asked whether the workers raised concerns about their conditions with their employers. 'Based on my observations, they are being brainwashed using religion,' Hasam said. 'The house leader always says, "Okay, please be patient, this is your test, coming to Australia, and one fine day you will get enough money. This is normal for everybody, and even me myself go through this process."'

The problems faced by other communities such as the Pacific Islanders on the federal government's Seasonal Worker Programme were akin to those of the backpackers, with undocumented workers working illegally the most exposed of all, especially since no amnesty existed for these people: they would be deported immediately should they be discovered. Backpackers are aware of this state of affairs, and often when they are working alongside undocumented workers they refuse to report infringements of their own rights because they know how vulnerable to deportation their fellow workers are. Most young travellers, like Mia, would side with the abused and disenfranchised over their oppressors, but are hamstrung from taking any meaningful action.

My own account started with what I had learnt the night before from Rob Clark, and then continued with as many transgressions as I knew about in the district of Mildura.

Andrew gave his speech about his girlfriend's situation, describing how he had told her 'that Australia has workplace and safety laws that can protect her'. He detailed her exploitation, the issues with piece rates, and said, 'I would love to tell you more, but my partner and her workmates are afraid that if I speak to you today not only will they lose their opportunity to stay in Australia, but they'll also be at risk of physical harm. For context, Queena's room was knocked on late at night and they were demanding which backpacker's boyfriend called the farm and company and got the union involved.'

He pointed out that farmers, hostels and contractors are taking advantage of backpackers of Asian backgrounds. 'There's a saying in China that the nail that sticks out gets hammered down, so traditionally it is not part of their culture to speak out against their employer.' He also mentioned how he had been turned down for work as an Australian, while Queena was offered the same job he'd been told was no longer available.

Andrew finished off with a poignant take on his own dismay:

Australia regards itself as the land of the fair go, but, having personally experienced what my partner is going through, and through working with Rosie, I can honestly say I no longer believe this to be true.

I rescue backpackers. The stories I have heard from very smart, intelligent young people from all over the world have made me disgusted, ashamed and embarrassed that I am an Australian.

Robyn told the inquiry of the main avenues she had explored to try to get help for backpackers, and how she had provided many of them with refuge in her house. 'My son, at that time, was working in Vienna in meteorological research. I thought, "Austria is looking after my son, so why isn't my country looking after these children from other countries?"'

The accounts that really seemed to affect the panel were those from the backpackers, as they were first-hand. Afterwards two members

of the panel approached Andrew and Laurent to apologise in
person for the way they had been treated on the 88 days scheme.
Locals who had attended in various official capacities expressed
their horror at what was happening in their area, and I realised that
modern slavery is a hidden crime that can occur under all of our
noses without visible signs.

My trip to Mildura had been proposed at the last minute. I had
written the speeches for the Salvos meeting and for the hearing
while on the road, and was happy that Andrew, Robyn and Laurent
had agreed to speak. All three had described typical scenarios of
exploitation, coupled in Andrew's case with the intimidation of his
girlfriend. I think between us we managed to get backpackers onto
the modern anti-slavery agenda.

Making a transglobal journey with very little preparation and
working constantly from the minute I hit the bitumen – having
barely slept on the flight over – is ill advised, especially at my age.
I decided that, in terms of public meetings and press work, I had
achieved the campaign objective of getting the word out there.
Yet on my return to the UK I had another speech to prepare. Paul
Broadbent of the Gangmasters and Labour Abuse Authority asked
me to speak at the GLAA's annual conference in October. Not
only did he want me to speak, but he wanted to make me the
keynote speaker.

Paul is one of those people you just want to make happy, and
so I said yes straight away, although I didn't understand why he
would want me to speak at such a prestigious event. Everyone in
the UK with an interest in the modern anti-slavery agenda would
be there. I was terrified, convinced I would make a fool of myself.

Mary Gaskin helped me to hone the speech in readiness for the big day.

Paul had asked for something quite emotive, with lots of pictures of Mia and Tom Jackson, so delivering it was tough. I had to stop every few moments, fight back the tears and take a deep breath before I could carry on. Paul correctly understood that the conference needed to get to the heart of the matter of labour exploitation, which is exactly where I was coming from.

What I wanted to express most of all is that modern slavery can touch all of our lives in unexpected ways. It's not something that's 'out there' and 'other'. Mia and Tom could not have been more treasured. They were both young and aspirational, with their lives ahead of them. But they were no different, no more or less special than any of the victims of exploitation, neglect and slavery any-where in the world, and their loss, despite all the press attention it had received, was no more or less poignant. Life matters, and the work being carried out by the Gangmasters and Labour Abuse Authority needs to be acknowledged, supported, and replicated far and wide.

I needn't have worried. My address wasn't just well-received – I got a standing ovation, and my Twitter feed later was gratifyingly full of praise. I hoped that sharing such a personal account would achieve the aims Paul envisaged and help those incredibly dedicated advocates – who might otherwise find themselves swamped in bureaucracy and the nitty-gritty of legislation – to reconnect with why they had become involved in the labour abuse agenda in the first place. I understood how much easier it might be for them to empathise with my loss than with those of victims from different backgrounds, but I knew they were wise and informed enough to recognise that my plight is replicated on a daily basis the world over.

17

Christmas

THE SECOND CHRISTMAS WITHOUT MIA, IN 2017, WAS SPENT WITH my cousin in Cambridgeshire, so I managed to get away without decorating the tree for another year. The Christmas was blighted by more death: I learnt that the charismatic, strong-willed force that was Paul Broadbent of the GLAA had taken his own life, leaving behind his wife and a beautiful little girl.

This man had been so thoughtful in the way he spoke to me, and so stalwart in his support, I just couldn't understand how he could do something that would have such a profound impact on those around him. Since then I think I have come to terms with the fact that I have no comprehension of where mental illness and depression can take you, and I am just eternally grateful that I was dealt a set of genes that precluded these curses. For a while after his death, darkness descended, and I felt an absence where previously there was a powerful source of strength.

By now, Stewart and I were pretty strong together, despite the road we'd travelled in what had been a relatively new relationship. We met in August 2013 and although we'd got along really well from the beginning, honestly I'd been unsure whether we would go the distance. I'd dated in the past, and the fact that I had resolutely put Mia first had always been a deal breaker when it came to anything lasting. But Stewart and I were similar in important ways. We had a shared sense of decency and self-respect, were both honest and hard grafters. We had been careful with money all our lives, but we were by no means well-off by the standards of most of my university friends. Neither of us were too hung up about that, though, as we enjoyed the simple pleasures – keeping dogs and chickens for example, long walks and the occasional trip away in the camper van. And as it transpired, Stewart understood from day one where he was in the pecking order!

Mia had been happy that I'd found a relationship with potential as she wanted me to settle down so she could travel, or even settle abroad, with a clear conscience. To my delight, after Stewart and I moved in together a year into the relationship, the two of them bonded over their silent resentment of the start of the day as they fumbled for keys and cups of coffee on dark winter mornings. The fact that I am a morning person only brought them closer together: 'Who in their right mind gets up with the lark at the weekend, exhibiting that insanely irritating joie de vivre? And as for hoovering? Isn't that actually illegal in the mornings? God give us strength!' I could drive them both mad before either of them even surfaced!

Stewart used to take Mia down to her stop to catch the bus to college. The two of them would either sit in absolute silence or have 80s rock music blaring at full volume while they smoked illicit cigarettes and sang their hearts out.

Once, in the early days, when Stewart and I had rowed and briefly parted company, Mia pointed out how much Stewart loved me, describing how, on his days off, he'd make dinner and put the kettle on just before I was due to arrive home, so he could have a cup of tea waiting as I came through the door. I realised she actually had a great deal of respect for Stewart, and wanted the relationship to work. That conversation was instrumental in bringing us back together. It still sees me through our occasional rows, as I realise Mia never wanted me to be alone.

More recently, the relationship had been strengthened by common ground. Stewart lost his only brother to suicide ten years before we met, and so he had supported his mother through her grief while struggling with his own personal sense of loss. For this reason he knew from the outset how long my journey was going to be, and he never wavered in his support. Additionally, although I think he sometimes saw the campaign as an irritant because it took me away from him, he was completely supportive, and even made time in the mornings to catch up on the latest news from Australia before he set off to work. His really good grasp of the issues meant he could quote you the finer points of the Australian immigration system without any problem!

For these and many more reasons, we were now starting to plan a wedding, which would take place some time in 2018. We were going round and round about where to hold it. Originally we wanted to get married in the chapel where Mia's life was commemorated on the Gold Coast, because we loved the place and wanted Mia to 'be there' with us. But I wasn't sure about this idea, as it would stop so many of our British friends from joining us, and there was a risk it would be heartbreaking to have those dark days so present during the ceremony.

After surviving Christmas, I decided we both needed a break, so I booked us flights to La Palma in the Canary Islands in February, and found a remote cottage for us to stay in on the southernmost tip of the island.

It seemed to me that I was surrounded by metaphors for my grief: a relatively young island, constantly in flux, La Palma was formed by volcanic eruptions, and the rock and earth were a mournful and dramatic black, battered by incredible Atlantic waves. It exuded a fearful sense of the danger of further eruptions, and yet everywhere this black earth gave way to the greenery of new life. The dark soil was incredibly fertile, yielding an abundance of nutritious fruit, while the azure blue sea is beautifully clean and teaming with marine life.

I felt like one of the black pebbles being polished by the Atlantic waves, honing my coping mechanisms, wondering where the next wave would take me. Always mindful that Mia could no longer live a long and full life, now my belief was that I was duty-bound to do this for her. When I looked at the beautiful gifts of life on earth, I looked as if through two pairs of eyes.

On our return home, Stewart, like many others in retail, was being threatened with redundancy, so we decided we needed to fill our coffers. Of course, campaigning doesn't bring in an income, so we weighed up various business ideas as a way of investing some of the small inheritance I'd received after Mum's death. Both of us had toyed with the idea of going into catering on retirement from our respective careers, and Stewart had trained as a chef some decades earlier. On a chance visit to some friends in Suffolk we came across a mobile pizza business, and we decided that this would be a template for our own.

It took just three months for us to pull everything together. Bella Mia would be a brightly painted horse float deployed to transport a wood-fired pizza oven around our local villages. Within days I'd found a suitably vintage horse float on eBay and dragged Stewart over to Sheffield to check it out. It was ancient and ugly, with more than a whiff of horse manure lingering. Before he could change his mind, I'd bargained the seller down to a less extortionate price (but nevertheless way over the odds) and we were on our way home! Stewart got to work pulling out the existing, somewhat decrepit, fixtures and replacing them with more compliant equipment, including a beautiful shiny new pizza oven.

The next problem was that neither of us had any clue about how to make a pizza! After watching numerous YouTube videos and much trial and error, followed by a second visit to Suffolk to discuss procedure with the Italian pizza chef whose business had since been purchased by our friends, we started to get the hang of it. In the early days we were painstakingly slow.

We found two permanent weekly pitches at local public houses, and then offered catering for weddings, local fetes and music festivals. It wasn't long before our business started to bring in a small income. More importantly, it got us out of the house, meeting people and socialising, but in a way that didn't involve having to engage in any in-depth conversation. I enjoyed the physical – almost meditative – aspects of creating the dough, kneading it and making the bases. It's repetitive, so takes very little thought. We cooked everything from scratch, for the pure satisfaction of nurturing others, but also for the therapy of having a routine and creating a good product. That said, Stewart and I had some explosive rows while we were trying to work through differences of opinion over the minutiae of the business – but we would always agree that it was because we both cared so much. We were incredibly busy everywhere we pitched up, so all in all it was shaping up to be a success.

18

The Hearing

DESPITE FEELING THAT WE WERE MOVING ON, THERE WAS AN
event hanging over us that remained unresolved, and that was
Ayad's trial.

From the early days I had understood that there was a distinct
probability that Ayad would be determined mentally ill at the time
of the killings, and that therefore he would not stand trial. The
time it took to ascertain whether this was indeed the case was also
understandable, given that mistakes had been made in the past –
people had been placed in mental health institutions when it was
later established that they were in fact perfectly in control of their
faculties and should have been tried in the criminal court. In fact,
the brother of one of my Australian contacts was one of these
people. A man had killed his girlfriend in an attack which was
assumed to be owing to his medical condition, but it subsequently
came to light that he'd been abusing her for a long time. Neither
the perpetrator's family nor the victim's had been allowed to speak

in the mental health courts, but they came forward with this evidence later and the killer was imprisoned. Stewart and I knew it was important that the courts get it right in Mia and Tom's case.

A date in April 2018 was set for the hearing in the Queensland District Court in Brisbane, for which we were invited to write witness statements. Mine was edited down to this:

Mia was full of light, laughter and fun. She was an absolute joy to be around, and she was loved by countless people both here in Derbyshire and around the world. Her friends in Australia organised a memorial for her, and her memorial in the UK was attended by people who had travelled from Turkey, Singapore and the United States. The tributes came from all over the world too, about how kind Mia was, how tolerant of others, how full of love for everyone she met, how she would stop and speak to mothers in the slums of Mumbai or Essaouira and play with their children, or dance with homeless people in the city streets in the UK. No one was too good for her, and no one too poor. She was just my living, laughing girl, always full of the joy of being alive.

The worst thing for me, apart from my own grief, was the anger and pain of the children she was closest to. They are still full of anger and pain, and there's nothing I can do personally to solve that. I hope it will ease with time, as they were too young to be faced with such brutality to their beloved Mia.

As for me, the loss has been a long ache, and many, many nights I lie awake, thinking about my daughter's last moments, and how it must have felt for her to lie dying. Did she feel pain? Did she know she was going? The images haunt me, waking and sleeping. I found my grief had a physical impact on my body, and I have gone from being an active person who took care of my physical and mental states to being literally crippled by grief: the effects of PTSD are taking their toll and manifesting in joint pain, exhaustion and tension. I no longer work as a teacher because I know I cannot face those rows of teenagers: constant reminders of my girl and her untimely death.

So how do I feel about the person who has been charged with Mia's murder?

Well, I certainly do not wish that person pain, or horror, or anguish. I don't want the person to rot in hell, and what happened has certainly not robbed me of my ability to appreciate the sanctity of life.

Nothing can undo what happened that night. However, I only wish that person and his family peace as once this person comes to realise what they have done, their internal suffering will be worse than anything that is imposed upon them.

I want everyone to understand, though, that this man's act of violence has robbed my world of my beloved daughter, a young girl who had everything to live for, who was loved by very many people, who had so much love in her heart to give to others. Mia was a sweet girl who would never hurt another intentionally, and would protect her friends from hurt if she could. She was feisty and caring, and believed in karma and in loving kindness. I am proud to have been her mother, and I will hold her in my heart until I die.

Nicola, Mia's half-sister, said she intended to go to Brisbane for the hearing. At first Les Jackson was adamant he didn't want to go because he wanted no part in the mental health court process; he was only interested in a criminal court trial. I didn't want to go but for other reasons: I couldn't see what good would come of it, and I had no desire to witness Ayad's suffering or to see justice being done.

Eventually I think Les and I each realised we weren't going to hear any evidence unless we were actually present at the hearing, so we both ended up going. I made the decision less than a week before the actual date, so had to endure another rushed intercontinental flight. Luckily I managed to book the same outgoing flights and hotel as Nicola, so at least we had each other for company.

The day dawned and I was awake very early, anticipating what was to come with many conflicting emotions. I was finally to encounter the man who had taken the life of my child. I hoped to find some sense of closure from that meeting. I didn't feel angry or afraid, but I felt loss, and pity, and a profound sense of dejection and grief for all the people who had suffered that awful night, not least Ayad himself. I had a pressing need to be alone in the hours before the court case, and I walked to the courtroom, trying to ease my aching heart and prepare myself for the day to come, and particularly for the encounter with this man who had figured so large in our imaginations for so many months.

As a group we were given some preferential treatment, having had so much media attention around the high-profile deaths and my subsequent campaign. Todd Fuller, the prosecution attorney, offered to meet us beforehand, along with our support worker from the Queensland Victim Support Service, Karen Harris. Todd made it very clear that the case was unlikely to be tried in the criminal courts.

A couple of things we did learn, however, were that Ayad's legal team was one of the best he could have had, and expensive. I was also told for the first time in the meeting with Todd that Mia had talked about wanting to change rooms in the hostel, so she was clearly uncomfortable with Ayad. This reduced me to tears, and I had to leave the room to calm down.

Recently I have received a report of the coroner's findings, which noted:

> I am of the view that unless a female has requested to sleep in mixed dormitories or bedrooms, best practice would be served by placing women with other women. Such high density sharing arrangements are already fraught, even without the added layer of vulnerability a woman may experience being accommodated with males not known to her. In Mia's case she was placed in a room with only two other males, one of whom was a stranger to her, had previously been involved in a confrontation with two other guests (which regardless of the circumstances would still have constituted a breach of the house rules), and had also put management on prior notice of his unwillingness to share the room with others. Whilst I accept management should retain the discretion as to how rooms are allocated, they should also bring some judgement to bear over which guests should or should not be housed together, not simply as a matter of convenience.

The coroner concluded, however, that: 'I am unable to conclude that Mia during her brief conversation with xxx on 22 August 2016 [. . .] made any disclosure to the effect of having requested a change of room that was refused.'

*

I awoke early with the birds, as I always did when I needed to connect spiritually with Mia. As I sat meditating I felt a strange sense
of calm descend, and I knew she was present. I had told Nicola the
night before that I would be walking to court alone, because I knew
I would need the headspace to prepare myself and to find strength
for the long day ahead. I was fearful of this man who had previously been considered too dangerous to appear in court because
of the savagery of his attacks on Mia and Tom, and his subsequent
aggression towards the police. But as I stilled myself in my hotel
room, superseding the fear was a need to find some way to connect
on a human level, and to find some degree of understanding of his
destructive spree that night.

The following day, placing my heels in my bag and donning a
pair of stout walking shoes, I headed to the court, feeling the warmth
of the late summer, and wondering whether Ayad would be denied
this feeling of pleasure from the elements that was my main source
of sustenance. Did I want him to be denied it? Would I prefer him
to be sentenced to life imprisonment? Still, the idea of justice provid-
ing some sort of closure for the victims was completely alien to me;
I couldn't see how I would ever benefit from another person's suffering, especially when that person was clearly mentally ill.

Les and I arrived early and hugged each other with that sense
of kinship which had become so important. Karen then turned up
and she sat with us over breakfast, explaining the procedure and
helping us to understand what the different roles of each partici-
pant were in the courtroom.

We waited for the man who had killed our children to appear,
fully expecting to see a huge, grinning, swaggering and testosterone-
driven monster. So when a somewhat wizened and broken-looking
man shuffled in, none of us really paid much attention until we

realised he was shuffling because his legs were in chains. The man we'd taken for a swaggering chest-beating cage fighter was here before us, depleted into a shadow. The eight policemen who accompanied him seemed to be overkill, until you thought back to his arrest and how many of the police officers had been injured that night.

He was placed in a large glass isolating box, with his interpreter placed outside it. He stared at his knees for the entire day, only looking up to nod to his interpreter to show he understood. He was much smaller than he looked in the photos we had seen, and he now appeared exhausted and depressed. He looked like someone in his mid-forties, not his early thirties. Later, Todd, the prosecuting attorney called him 'a broken man', and I had to agree.

The proceedings were as we had been told: all about his mental-health issues. The reason it had taken so long to get to this point was because he had been assessed in a high-security mental-health unit. He arrived at that correctional institution in August 2016 in a state of terror. He apparently believed that nearly everyone at Home Hill Backpackers was in a conspiracy to try to kill him, although he did say he liked Mia and Tom, so could see no reason for having attacked them.

The facts are that after he killed her, Ayad dived head-first from the balcony and landed on his upper back, breaking vertebrae in his back and neck. He said he believed he killed Tom in self-defence. During his arrest, he attacked a number of policemen, as he believed they were trying to kill him too. After he was arrested, he refused food and medication, and had to be kept alive through forced feeding for months. His condition did not improve even when he stopped using cannabis and he was kept in isolation as he believed the medical staff were trying to kill him. His mental state had been stabilised through medication.

I knew many people were wishing him and his family pain, and anguish and even death. I understood their thoughts.

As the hearing progressed through the day, one of the psychiatrists asked about witness reports from backpackers who had said that Ayad had been obsessed with Mia, that he had talked about her as if she had been his possession. As she spoke, the psychiatrist indicated a file full of evidence and said, 'There are numerous eyewitness accounts which suggest this is the case.' I felt the judge was dismissive, claiming that the accounts had been fabricated after the event and were therefore invalid, because the backpackers would have spoken to each other and attributed motives to Ayad which didn't actually exist. She did, however, acknowledge that Ayad believed Mia had been put in his room in order to keep him at the hostel.

I was shocked. It seemed to me that the only witness who was to be believed was Ayad, a man who had every reason to lie in order to stay out of prison. Meanwhile, anything that suggested he might have had a motive was to be disregarded as the workings of deranged minds, even though the young people concerned were in agreement that he had been obsessed with Mia. His own account was that he had no interest in her, she was just 'a silly little girl'. Well Mia could be silly, and she was petite, but according to the press, Ayad had been obsessed with a media personality who was very similar in appearance to Mia, and I had heard many accounts of how he obsessed over her from eye witnesses.

At this point I became furious. I stood up muttering and left the courtroom, with a cursory nod to the judge. I flew into the lobby to vent and found two policemen idling out there, waiting for their lunch.

'This is a complete waste of time, the whole thing is a set-up!' I started. 'So-called independent witnesses? They've concocted the whole thing together to avoid a criminal case! Australia doesn't want justice! This is the cheap option . . . they want to repatriate him so they don't have to treat him, and then the French will just release him . . .'

I was at the point of implicating the Turnbull administration, the French government and the UK High Commission. And then suddenly I realised what was happening to me. I was developing a paranoid, delusional conspiracy theory in my head which was taking me along the path Ayad himself had trod. It was a dark place. I was angry, and I knew I could go as far as I wanted down that path and it would never get any lighter.

So I stopped, and I reconnected with who I am, and who Mia was. And I went back into the court, and heard the verdict, and I recognised that the judge was trying her damnedest to ensure Ayad was kept for a minimum term of ten years. She said she acknowledged he must be on medication and off cannabis for the rest of his life, because cannabis for him was the trigger for schizophrenia. (He'd been smoking it since he was twelve years old, and this was his first episode.) To be perfectly honest, I didn't feel as if any of it was my problem anyway. I have no more children to lose.

Although the proceedings now were devoted to the technicalities of Ayad's treatment, Les Jackson and I were allowed to read out our victim impact statements. Ayad continued to stare at his knees, occasionally looking up at his interpreter to nod his affirmation of having understood – apart from once, when I talked about his realisation of what he had done as being worse than anything that could be inflicted on him. At that point he looked at me, and we stared at each other in silence for a count of three. I felt that the fact I refused to vent about hating him had made an impact. And I then realised that this was why I had flown half way around the world and barely slept for five days – in the hope of achieving that connection. To my mind, it's only through those moments of connection and understanding, when you experience a moment of insight into the mind of another being, that change can be initiated.

In her summing up, the judge passed a message back to Les and me from Ayad expressing his grief for what he had done to Mia and Tom, and the fact that he cried every day when he recollected that fact. I really do believe that to live with having taken the lives of two people must be a life sentence in itself.

Prior to entering court I had written this letter to Ayad's mother:

> Family members present in court would like to convey our
> deepest sympathies to you. We understand that your suffering
> is not dissimilar to ours and we bear no ill will to you. If you
> would like to meet and talk parent to parent I would be happy
> for that to happen.

She was not in court, but at the beginning of the proceedings her liaison officer gave me her response:

> We share your immense pain and grief because I am a mother
> first and foremost, but words are too weak to ask for forgive-
> ness. My son has never been aggressive, violent or nasty in his

past life. He was a peaceful and respectful boy and now he is portrayed as a monster.

Our suffering, thinking what he has done, will never end. It is a nightmare. May you one day find peace in your hearts.

At the end of the trial I found his mother's liaison officer again and asked her that she give my contact details to Ayad's mother, so that we could meet if she would like to.

Since making that decision the words of an incredible woman, Eva Mozes Kor, have been brought to my attention. Eva, along with her twin, Miriam, was subjected to human experimentation by Josef Mengele at Auschwitz. On becoming a forgiveness advocate, she would talk about writing a letter to the Nazi doctor Hans Munch, who signed death certificates for those murdered in the gas chambers. After persuading him to sign a document at Auschwitz admitting what had happened there, Kor was moved to write him a letter of forgiveness. 'What I discovered for myself was life-changing. I discovered that I had the power to forgive. No one could give me that power, and no one could take it away. It was all mine to use in any way I wished.' As a victim of what had occurred at Auschwitz almost fifty years before, Eva never realised she had any power over her own life.

Whether or not people thought I was mad for being able to forgive, I didn't care, because it was consistent with Mia's own values since she was a little girl. We both believed that you can only move on in life through love and forgiveness, which was the path she tried so hard to tread herself.

*

Now, as I'm further down my own journey of forgiveness, while I'm at peace with Ayad and his family, I can't help but wonder what evidence remained unheard because of the way the court proceedings went.

Credible witnesses told me that Ayad was obsessed with Mia and believed she belonged to him. Daniel Richards, who worked with Ayad in the field and who was with Mia when she died, insists that Ayad had objected to Mia showing pictures of herself to others in the hostel. (The pictures he was talking about were a set of nude studies taken by a professional photographer. I am grateful to the photographer that he never shared them with the press or on social media after her death, but I'm not surprised that Mia showed them off among her backpacker friends because they are truly gorgeous pictures of a young woman at the height of her youth and beauty. I have copies myself and treasure them.)

I would like to have had these and other details of Ayad's increased interest in Mia explored further in court, along with who Mia told about her concerns. The coroner has since reported:

By various accounts, the timing of Mia's arrival aligns with a change in Ayad's character and behaviour, and the evidence supports a view that Ayad developed a focus on Mia. The evidence suggests that the only interaction between Ayad and Mia arose in the context of the shared room, they were otherwise not known to socialise or work together. Mr Matteo Bellusci, an Italian national who was staying at the Hostel at the time of Mia and Mr Bower's arrival, recalled a conversation with Ayad in the kitchen area of the Backpackers. Mr Bellusci deposed as follows: '[Ayad] told me that he thought Mia was wonderful and that she has a good body and that when he leaves he will take Mia with him. [Ayad] said to me that Mia is his wife. I did not think this made sense because he is not Mia's husband or boyfriend'. Another guest, Ms Josie Bennett, a UK national, recalled a separate conversation she had with three other male guests (one of whom was Ayad) about one week prior to the events on 23 August 2016. This would have likely been very shortly after the time Mia and Mr Bowers arrived. Mia's name came up in conversation amongst the male guests, although she was not present. Ayad commented: 'Yeah but she is in my room, she is my wife, I want to sleep with her'. I note that when Ms Bennett heard that comment she observed the other male guests 'shrug it off' and not say anything to Ayad. The comments were a matter of concern to Ms Bennett. The comments made by Ayad and his actions towards her were demonstrative of a sexual interest towards Mia. In circumstances where Ayad and Mia had only been known to each other for an extremely short period of time and had limited interactions with each other I consider these behaviours should have caused serious concern to those who either heard or potentially observed them.

I am not informed of whether Mia was made directly aware of these comments or whether they were raised with any of the staff at the Hostel. However had Mia been made aware of the comments Ayad was making to others, it may have further alerted her and confirmed the concerns she herself held about him.

The coroner said in summary: 'I am unable to conclude that Mia during her brief conversation with xxx on 22 August 2016

[. . .] made any disclosure to the effect of being sexually assaulted or harassed by Ayad.'

Regardless of whether Mia did or did not tell the hostel about her concerns, it is my view that hostels in general should have a duty of care towards their guests. There should be a 'fit and proper' test for hostel owners in Australia. A hostel's owners should be responsible if their accommodation is awash with drugs or alcohol; they should not be able to advertise heavily on social media to attract people to the hostel when work is scarce; or take advantage of people made vulnerable by their need to complete their 88 days.

19

Festival of Light

THURSDAY, 28 JUNE 2018 WAS A BIG DAY, AS CHRIS CREWTHER MP read and introduced Australia's first Modern Slavery Bill to parliament. It was intended to tackle crimes that should not occur in the twenty-first century, such as sexual slavery, orphan trafficking, debt bondage, forced labour, forced marriage, servitude and more. But without enforcement, the bill would lack teeth, and there were still no moves afoot in Australia to create a body with the kind of powers held by the Gangmasters and Labour Abuse Authority in the UK.

News was also breaking about a Fair Work Ombudsmen report into employment practices within the horticulture and viticulture industries of the Harvest Trail to be released later that year. It would show evidence of exactly what I'd been claiming since Mia's and Tom's deaths, that there is widespread abuse of backpackers. One article quoted UTS senior law lecturer Laurie Berg: 'This survey shows us that we have a really large silent underclass of invisible temporary workers who are being paid well below the minimum wage.'

Alongside this news I received a message on social media from Jill Biddington, a union organiser who had been supportive of the campaign since watching *Australian Story*, saying that she had seen Mia in a dream, and that Mia was writing 'I love you Mum' in white stones on the sand. She said she thought she'd met Mia, and that she was at peace. We talked on Messenger about the campaign, and I asked her whether she thought we'd achieved anything so far. Her response was heartening.

> I wonder if without you and the campaign we would have the Labour Hire legislation. I don't think so. Nor do I think we would have the same result on the inquiry into modern slavery. I think I might still be struggling to convince the union movement about the problems caused by exploitation of working holiday-makers. I think we would still have a huge divide.

She also spoke of her embarrassment for Australia and said, 'I have never worried so much for a stranger as I have for you.'

It was wonderful to hear this, and I felt she was right, things were moving, but that we had a long way to go.

We also received the news on 28 June that Ayad's sentence would not be subjected to a ten-year non-revocation order, a relatively new legal power available to the mental health courts which would prevent Ayad from being released before the ten years was up. This was probably the humane way forward, as for Ayad to recover it made sense for his family to be able to visit him. Nevertheless, some people thought questions still remained unanswered. Had he been temporarily insane? Had he lied to the court and was in fact infatuated with Mia and killed her because he couldn't have her? Either way he now needed to live with what he'd done.

A few months later, our wedding went so smoothly it was almost as if an invisible hand were guiding us. Stewart and I were given a perfect window of November sunshine in a week where the rain had lashed the Derbyshire hills mercilessly. A number of friends and I walked uphill in a kind of procession to join Stewart at Mia's bench. I was wearing a pair of fur-lined Timberland boots, which Mia had bought for me and I adored. Denise, a close friend, blessed us in a very moving personalised unofficial service. We drank mead from a goblet while tearful friends watched on. It felt right to have the wedding blessed in the hills where Mia had spent so much time.

The wedding ceremony itself, held at a stylish converted cotton mill in our town, was packed with family and friends, and the feeling of goodwill was palpable. I think the general consensus was that we'd earned some happiness.

Most moving for me was the presence of friends who made monumental efforts to join us, including fellow campaigners from Australia, Alison Rahill and her husband Matt Pulford. I had rented a beautiful old house in Wirksworth for all the travelling guests so they would be as comfortable as possible.

I'd invited a number of Mia's friends and was really touched that they turned up to celebrate with us. One of their number was Mia's beloved friend and travelling companion from Thailand, Anna Boo, who flew in from Copenhagen where she had been studying. When Mia first posted pictures of herself and Anna Boo I was struck by their similarity – they both had Asian and European blood – but more striking were their joyous smiles and a sense of fun which made them look like kin. I'd been delighted that Mia had met Anna and they'd formed a bond so quickly. Later Anna told me that Mia had arrived in town on the day of the full moon festival and not been able to find anywhere to stay, so Anna had given her the spare bed in her hotel room. The girls had got so close in just one week that when Mia said goodbye, Anna chased after her to give her a parting gift and had found Mia in tears. They were reunited in Bali, and their friendship strengthened over a Christmas spent together on the beach, along with Alice, a close friend of Mia's from home.

After Mia died I was surprised by two simultaneous texts. I had given Mia's phone to her cousin Aoife for safekeeping, and she was therefore aware of incoming messages. She suddenly texted me one morning saying, 'Is it weird that Anna Boo still messages Mia?' At exactly the same moment Anna messaged to say, 'I still send messages to Mia, I feel so close to her, is that wrong?'

Anna wasn't able to attend either of Mia's memorial services, and two years after her death she was still saying she wasn't coping with Mia's death. I felt she had missed a vital part of the grieving process, which is communion with others who love your lost one, so I was delighted when she accepted our wedding invitation.

I felt so grateful to her for coming, it was like a piece of Mia had arrived back in Derbyshire, but I didn't realise how important it was to her until I read the note she'd left me.

I hope you know how much this means to me. Sometimes life is full of nonsense, but today I understand everything clearly. The time spent with our loved ones is precious and has to be lived fully. I want you to know that we are all changed forever by who Mia was and what she means to us. It was so hard for

me to let her go after a week. It's too hard for me to let her go
for all time. You remind me of her so much, as I remind you of
her. Special, isn't it?

I will see you in Copenhagen.

Love,

Anna.

Stewart and I spent our honeymoon in Thailand, again
booked on a whim. We had two weeks on a romantic retreat in
Krabi, a holiday of warmth, empty beaches and great food. On
22 November we headed into Krabi and took a boat ride out to
one of the islands offshore, where we shared a day on a beach with
a delightfully naughty monkey. In the evening we were drawn to a
waterside bar and played a game of pool before deciding to take
a seat by the water. I was lost in deep thought about Mia, missing her terribly and overwhelmed with an inexplicable sense of loss
and sadness, such as I hadn't experienced for some time. Stewart
was chatting away and noticing things around him, as he is wont
to do. As the waiter appeared with what looked like a table decoration he said, 'That's what those women were making earlier, out of
banana leaves and flowers!' The decoration was intricate and very
pretty, orange flowers nestled among blue-green leaves which were
folded into the shapes of roses. The colours were those we'd used to
represent Mia since her death, and I smiled at the coincidence.

Suddenly Stewart said, 'Look, they're launching little boats into
the water!'

We looked out to sea and there were myriad little light boats
floating on the water. Stewart put two and two together and realised
the boats were actually what we had mistaken for table decorations,
so with permission we took ours to the nearby beach and launched

it into the water. We waded into the sea after it fully clothed and got drenched in the process, but it meant we could launch it properly and make sure the candle stayed alight.

The whole process felt so right, as if we were somehow making a special connection with Mia, but I didn't realise why until our return to the UK. I was sitting thinking about Anna and Mia and how they met, and remembered Anna's story about Mia at a festival of light and how she hadn't been able to find anywhere to stay. When I examined Mia's photos I found that she had indeed been at the Loi Krathong in Chiang Mai. Stewart and I just happened to pick that week to visit Thailand, completely unaware that we would experience the festival too. I knew then that this was a place I could go to find Mia again, and spend time making memories in her name. I was filled with love for Mia and Stewart, and a sense of gratitude that I'd been a mother to one beautiful person, and was now wife to another.

We arrived back from our honeymoon in December to the news that Australia now had a Modern Slavery Act! This was achieved through the work of a huge team of politicians, led by Chris Crewther MP, Senator Linda Reynolds and Lisa Singh MP as well as leading civil rights activists Alison Rahill, Jenny Stanger and Heather Moore. It meant that at last slavery was officially illegal in Australia, and also that there was recognition that it existed not just in their overseas supply chains, but domestically. The latter was down to the efforts made by survivors of slavery, including my good friend and constant ally Moe Turaga, who had addressed the regional hearing in Mildura with harrowing tales of mistreatment in Australia's fruit and vegetable industry.

I was proud to have been a part of that hearing, and to have ensured that backpacker stories and voices were heard, and that the worst aspects of the 88 days program were exposed for what they are: effectively, state-sponsored modern slavery for which Australia needs to be held accountable.

But this was just a beginning, and, as with all legislation, enforcement is everything. My view is that there is still a pressing need for Australia to create an enforcement agency, along the lines of the UK's Gangmasters and Labour Abuse Authority to provide a one-stop reporting system for all victims of exploitation and modern slavery, with officers given powers of arrest working closely with the police. Punishments need to be increased so that the crime of exploitation is no longer worth the risk for perpetrators, and a manslaughter charge needs to be introduced where culpability is proven for a workplace death.

However, the act was a significant moment, and a crucial part of Tom and Mia's legacy. It means that my daughter, and the brave man who tried to save her life, did not die in vain.

Postscript

LOOKING BACK, I WONDER WHETHER ANY PART OF ME KNEW THAT I'd never see Mia again when she left home. Was there a sense of premonition? Maybe, because the following week, Stewart and I talked about the worst-case scenario of her dying on the trip, and I told him that if anything happened to her I wouldn't be able to carry on. He replied that he agreed, he didn't think I'd be able to survive her death either.

Survival for me was down to the support I received from our community. I felt a sense of understanding and deep sympathy from family, friends and strangers alike, and was deeply comforted by the outpouring of feeling for dear Mia.

Loss, however, does not necessarily evoke such sympathy, and I've often wondered how it would have been if Mia had passed away quietly through illness, a drug overdose, accidental death or suicide. Or if I'd lost her to a long prison sentence? Would I have received the same support? Or would I have been made aware in sly ways of a communal judgement on my parenting?

Regardless of how a loved one passes from our lives, the pain is enormous and survivors need unconditional love, however it's expressed. Even if you 'can't find the words' it's important to try. Mostly, there really are no words, but when you're in a desperate place, you feel people's care as a healing balm. Just letting the bereaved know you care is enough. Cards, flowers, little acts of kindness all add up. In the end, we too will be remembered for the love we give, and this could be our only chance of immortality. My absolute favourite biblical quote is: 'Judge not, lest you be judged'.

There is no way to quantify or compare grief. Grieving the death of an animal, a parent, a grandparent is all poignant. The difference when a parent is grieving for a child is that the grief for a child doesn't really lessen with time; if anything it is augmented. So many, many painful reminders, so many missed moments, so much wasted potential. It doesn't go away, but it can be assimilated into who you are, for good or bad.

Here in the West we have an expectation that our children will outlive us. I was told over and over that my grief was justified because Mia had died before me and this was in some sense the wrong order. We seem to suffer a profound sense of injustice when this happens. But the words I hear Mia say most often, which ring on through the years are these: 'Suck it up, Momma!'

It also helps me to keep a global perspective. Across the world many lose their children, their families, their villages in one fell swoop. Children are having their lives destroyed by traffickers and other criminals as they attempt to reach safety on a daily basis. Some have the ability to survive all of this, while others go under. I wanted to join those survivors and live on for Mia. And I wanted to use the knowledge I have gained through her death to make a difference for others.

I have certainly changed. I think all parents will be aware that along with the pride and joy which is a big part of parenting, comes a concomitant sense of self-doubt, and often guilt. Did I work too hard and forget her needs? Should I have spent more on her, should I have indulged her less? Should I have been someone other than who I am? The 1970s concept of the 'good enough' parent, conceived by Donald Winnicott, always helped me to assuage the guilt of parenthood, but like almost every parent I know self-doubt is ever present.

And while the worry may diminish, the guilt of a grieving parent endures and destroys so many lives. However the child dies, you wonder and wonder what you could have done differently to prevent the death. You are stretched on a rack of guilt which can destroy your life, and eventually your very essence. I have seen that guilt in others, and feel the path I took may have been an attempt to combat that feeling. I couldn't bring my laughing girl home, but I could do my damnedest to ensure other children walked back through other doors.

I have done what I can over the past four-and-a-half years to honour my daughter and Tom Jackson, and to prevent more injury, abuse and loss of life on this ill-conceived scheme. It has been a long and often painful journey, and one I wish I never had to make. Nevertheless, knowing what I now know, I believe I had no other alternative than to follow the path I did, and I hope it has made a difference.

Many people have commented on how proud Mia would have been to see the campaign, the website and the media work I've carried out in her name. She would definitely have teased me about it that's for sure, but she had a sense of outrage, shared by youth generally, for anything she considered to be unfair or unjust, and she had a kindness and wisdom well beyond her years. Everything I have done has been through consultation with her spirit, and I've felt her guidance more than once when I have had to decide between different paths.

Sometimes I miss my girl terribly, but if I stop and allow myself the time to consider, often I find she was with me all along.

Acknowledgements

I would like to thank the following people:

Daniel Richards, for holding my daughter Mia while she died, for which I am eternally indebted.

For the immense and invaluable help they've given me in editing this book:

Sophie Ambrose and Clive Hebard in Australia and Helen Mangham and Charlotte Cole in the UK.

I would also like to thank Jennifer Feller for her tireless work on *Australian Story* and for believing in me when I was full of doubt, and Alison Rahill and Matt Pulford for putting me up, putting up with me and always being politically on point. Love you guys!

On the campaign front, thank you to Sir Kevin Hyland, Menna Rawlings and Kasandra Perry at the Foreign and Commonwealth Office, as well as Andrew Bretherton and Robyn Horvath in Australia and Mary Gaskin in the UK for your help with the campaign and your hard work on behalf of the migrant worker community.

Friends who have stood by me are too numerous to mention, but to list a few:

Sandra and Les Jackson for being supportive friends throughout.

My dear friends Rachel Fisher and Sine Fiennes in the UK, and Jesse Tawhi and Jayne in Australia.

And last but by no means least, thank you to Stewart Cormack, for always being there and for helping me pull through.

Resources

If any issues have come up while reading this book, or if you or anyone you know needs help, you can contact the following organisations.

Mental health support services

Lifeline: 13 11 14
lifeline.org.au

Beyond Blue: 1300 22 4636
beyondblue.org.au

headspace: 1800 650 890
headspace.org.au

ReachOut: au.reachout.com

Suicide Call Back Service: 1300 659 467
suicidecallbackservice.org.au

GriefLine: 1300 845 745
griefline.org.au

Australian Centre for Grief and Bereavement: grief.org.au

Support for temporary agricultural workers

Safe Work Australia
safeworkaustralia.gov.au/migrant-workers

Tom and Mia's Legacy

Further information on the campaign to raise awareness and prevent backpacker exploitation can be found at the following sites:

chuffed.org/project/tom-mias-legacy

facebook.com/tomandmiaslegacy

Discover a
new favourite